RESPECTING THE LORD

The True Beginning of Knowledge

From award winning author
Mark Stephen Taylor

*For since the creation of the world His invisible attributes,
His eternal power and divine nature, have been clearly
seen, being understood from what has been made, so that
men are without excuse*

(Romans 1:20 NASB)

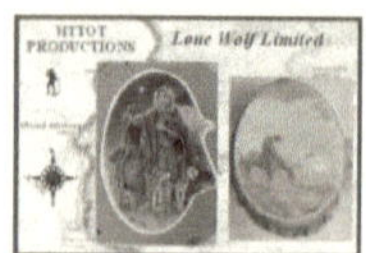

RESPECTING THE LORD

The True Beginning of Knowledge

There does not seem to be a predominant amount of respect for the Lord in these current times in which we live. Let's face it —it's a chaotic world out there, is it not? I would blame most of that on a lack of both teaching and understanding regarding the Creator of the world. However, the existence of God can be clearly seen through the things He has made, which things are quite obvious all around us Yet, it appears that many are not really looking. Why is that, I wonder?

It is written that a fear (respect) of the Lord is truly the beginning of knowledge (Proverbs 1:7). Here, Solomon is clearly teaching that belief in God is the necessary prelude to the understanding of solid truth and the acquisition of any knowledge. *Beginning* is literally first in order of importance; the first principle. In many Biblical passages the fear (respect) of the Lord is to be taught and learned. The beginning (foundation) of all true knowledge is grounded in this respect.

The purpose of this particular writing is to teach one how and why to respect the Lord. It is an eye-opening hike along the trail of truth which can give understanding to the simple—to those of contrite heart. To anyone who has the ability to reason this journey will be quite profoundly informative. This journey requires courage—the personal will to reach the summit of the mountain of believing. We are hoping, dear reader, that you are one of those rare persons...

Sincerely, M S Taylor and The HTTOT Staff

From

LONE WOLF LIMITED

A Division of *M S Taylor Productions*
1997-Present
PO Box 547 Lone Pine, CA, 93545
Phone 909-549-0068

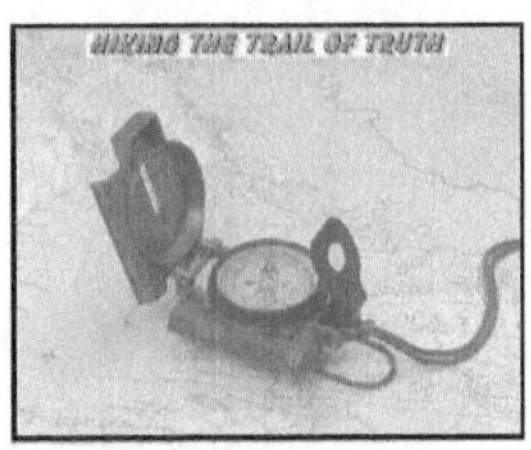

Vol. 1: Hiking the Trail of Truth: Knowing God Through His Creation
Vol. II: Hiking Life's Difficult Trails: A Spiritual Journey
Vol. III: Hiking Life's Difficult Trails: High Country Hiker's Edition
Vol. IV: Knowing Just Who You Are: Educating Body, Mind, & Spirit
Vol. V: Something Has Come Between Us: A Treatise on Your
Relationship with God
Vol. VI: Mountain Meditations: A Daily Spiritual Journey for Hikers
Vol. VII: The Last Trumpet: The Truth Concerning Wold End Events
Vol. VIII: A Broken Spirit, A Contrite Heart
Vol. IX: Respecting the Lord: The True Beginning of Knowledge
Vol. X: ILLUMINATION: A Hike into the High Country
Vol. XI: Walk Before Me: Your Daily Walk With God
Vol. XII: Human Nature: Our Struggle with Good and Evil

Additional books available from this author; see page 139

Dedication:

This entire writing is dedicated to those most sincere folk's who
would like to have a truly deeper understanding of life…

In memory of

Pauline Evelyn Boley Taylor
1918-1959

Sincerely, *Mark S Taylor*

About the Author

Mr. Taylor was educated in criminal psychology and geology, and is currently a Biblical teacher and counselor. His award-winning autobiography, '*Hiking the Trail of Truth*', is perhaps one of the most informative books ever written on the subject of 'knowing God through His creation'. Each of his varied works, both fiction and non-fiction alike, have generated outstanding reviews. He's quite often out there; hiking and exploring somewhere in the west, and always working on something new—for our benefit.

Since his retirement from law enforcement in 1994, he has hiked much of the High Sierra mountain range of California and explored the vast deserts of the American Southwest. He has also spent time among the Native Americans. His experiences and knowledge have earned him a writing style that is indeed unique. His book tours also allow him to meet with many people on a personal level, and share with them his obvious wisdom and insight.

Information on contacting Mr. Taylor personally can be found within any of his books. He claims to be nobody special, and loves to hear from his readers.

RESPECTING THE LORD
The True Beginning of Knowledge

Chapter One: **The X Files**

We live in a time when it seems that our learning institutions fall short of teaching ethical/moral principles to students—from grade school levels and on through college. For me, having been born in 1945, it's hard in this day and age to imagine such drastic changes in what is being taught. History, English, science, mathematics, speech, civics, religion and personal one-on-one communication have all been pushed aside and seemingly replaced with computer technology, I-phone mania, and social media propaganda of all sorts.

Most of us senior folk's are asking ourselves, 'what the heck has happened here?' Not only has technology changed, but personal attitudes and moral values have changed as well—taken a jump right off the edge of a cliff. None of us are perfect, but many have ceased even trying to be. I ask myself, 'do people now-a-days know who they really are—where they are going?' After considerable deep thought on the matter my conclusion was that they must have no knowledge or understanding of the One who formed them.

Have they not heard? Have they not read? For since the creation of the world His invisible attributes, His eternal power and divine nature, have been clearly seen, being understood from what has been made, so that men are without excuse (Romans 1:20). The bottom line is of course that a *disciplined encounter* with true wisdom (respect for the Lord) will produce a perceptive spirit. The senses will be exercised to discern both good and evil. That discernment, when yoked with instruction, produces itself in justice, judgment, and equity.

The first of those three terms (justice) describes that which is fitting according to the will of the supreme Judge, the second (judgment) that which is customarily considered good among men, and the third (equity) that which is straightforward, honorable, and upright. It is not only the young who will profit from this encounter, but the wise, through careful attention, will increase their learning. They will be able to guide themselves and others across the troubled waters of this life.

Naturally it is hard for many to unlearn what they have learned with respect to the myriad of negative things that we may have been taught all of our lives. Yet, a respect for the Lord will indeed require the renewing of one's mind (Romans 12:2). There are a multitude of false teachings about the Lord throughout the world today, just as there were over 2000 years ago (at the time of Christ) and even before that. Most people are prone to follow false teachings from both charismatic and traditional leaders. This is unfortunately human nature, but it does not have to be that way—the truth is out there, if one independently desires to seek it.

Again, I don't see a great overall respect for the Lord in the world today. The United States however was founded on the principle that God was our creator, and that He gave us the right to pursue life, liberty and happiness. He was indeed respected then—at least by those who initiated our founding principles. Today the people, for the most part, have forgotten the loyalty of the founding fathers and their principles of faith and justice—their respect for God. This is of course due to a modern day lack of true knowledge—a lack of understanding the divine.

Let us therefore expand your current knowledge at this time through initially (firstly) taking a look at some physical evidence. *Note*: I have chosen to designate this very first chapter the *X-files* of the book—you may choose to not believe what I am about to tell you along this journey, but I can assure you that everything that's talked about in this chapter *is out there*—I've seen the evidence—I've been there.

These *X-files* however have *nothing* to do with little green men in flying saucers. I only label them *X-files* because of the unbelievable measure of doubt surrounding their existence. With that same regard (doubt surrounding its truth), many people today consider the Bible to be the *X-files*. To the contrary the Bible is a great treasure. Its references to historical events, characters, and physical locations are absolutely correct. Gear up for an illuminating hike...

The photograph associated with this chapter (page 9) is an actual photo (taken by me) of the 5000-year-old remains of Noah's Ark as it appeared in 1991. Take a good look at it, dear reader, and let not your heart be troubled—be instead joyous! Go ahead—stick your tongue out at the skeptics and the non-believers—those without spiritual discernment.

The Ark is located some 8 miles southeast of Dogubayazit

on the *mountains of Uratu* (Ararat) in eastern Turkey, about 10 miles from the Iranian border. The Ark rests at a 6,300-foot elevation on the northward slope of a mountainous ridge, some 14 miles south of Mt. Ararat itself. In 1959, a NATO survey pilot took the first aerial photo of this site showing an incredible outline of a ship, high on a mountainside in a mud flow.

His discovery caused quite a stir. Newspapers in Turkey and the United States carried the story that year, and in the summer of 1960 an archaeological team from the U.S. mounted an expedition to the site. The team spent two days there, and upon finding no wood or obvious artifacts indicating the remains of a ship, reported at a news conference that they felt the object was likely only 'a natural formation.' Photographs of the expedition were carried in a story by Life magazine in September of 1960.

This first expedition however did not truly understand *what* to expect—they were looking for an intact ship, not the mere outline of a ship, nor the petrified remains of the vessel that were hidden beneath tens of feet of soil and rock. Nearly 5000 years of weathering had indeed camouflaged its true identity from this early summer 1960 team of apparently liberal or 'surface-thinking' archaeologists.

Incredibly, yet typical of an unbelieving world, no one returned for any further investigation until 1977, when the late, Biblical archaeologist Ron Wyatt and his two sons made the trip. Wyatt returned again in 1979, and made two more visits in 1984. Based on his observations he was fully persuaded that the site contained the remains of Noah's Ark. The main difficulty in proving this claim in 1977 was that the majority of the boat shaped object was buried beneath tens of feet of soil and rock—the result of a massive mudslide in the area.

But then, in late 1978, an earthquake caused the soil surrounding the object to fall away from its sides. With the soil removed from its outer surface, the object took on the more recognizable shape of a boat, which is *obvious* in the 1991 photograph on page 9. The general consensus of theologians and skeptics is of course that the Ark was supposed to have landed on the top of Mt. Ararat—how could it be 14 miles away at a lower elevation?

First of all, the Bible says that the Ark came to rest "upon the *mountains* of Ararat"—plural. The word in the Hebrew text translated Ararat is *Uratu*, which was an ancient kingdom in the region. Furthermore, many early historians attest that the remains of the Ark were visible in their day and could be visited on a routine basis by travelers who journeyed through the area.

For example, Berosus, a 3rd century BC Babylonian historian, says, "But of this boat that grounded in Armenia some part still remains in the mountains of the Gordyaeans (Kurds) in Armenia, and some get pitch from the boat by scraping it off and using it for amulets." The famous 1st century historian, Josephus, mentions that a plant called *amomum* grew in abundance at the Ark site. Amomum grows prolifically today on and around the site discovered by the NATO pilot.

Travelers could not have routinely visited the Ark if it were on the 16,946-foot summit of Mt. Ararat, nor can amomum grow in the ice and snow at that elevation. Furthermore, *common sense* tells us that many animals leaving the Ark would not have been physically able to descend the steep slopes of Mt. Ararat itself. Ark hunters today are still searching Mt. Ararat, apparently not even considering God's concern for the disembarking of the animals, nor the fact that the Bible does not put the boat's resting place upon that particular mountain.

In 1985, David Fasold, an expert on ancient ships who was quite aroused by Wyatt's discoveries, explored the Ark site with metal detectors. Tests conducted by Fasold and his associates indicated that there were lines of metal underground at the site. These lines are thought to represent rows of nails or spikes. They form a specific pattern both lengthwise and across the structure. The ones running lengthwise converge at points at either end of the site—clearly consistent with the construction of a large boat.

Also, the visible shape indicates that the structure is quite obviously the remains of a boat. Physical evidence in the surrounding area suggests that the Ark came to rest several hundred or perhaps as much as 1000 feet higher in elevation, and was later carried to its present location by a mudslide. It appears to have grounded on an upward protruding outcrop of bedrock. During the course of the mudslide the interior of the boat was filled with mud and rock.

This pressure would have caused the sides to be forced outward, resulting in the splayed condition of the structure now visible. The bedrock outcrop on which the boat grounded is now exposed at the surface, extending from the west side approximately to the center. The surveyed metal lines bend sharply around the rock outcrop. This suggests that the boat's bottom structure was damaged when it struck the rock. The starboard (right) side of the boat was most likely facing the outcrop during the mudslide when it was forced into it.

When the boat struck the outcrop, a portion of its lower midsection impaled itself on the rock. The mudslide continued to move the stern (rear) portion of the boat 90 degrees or more in the natural down slope direction of the slide. This movement continued to damage the boat, the rock pinnacle grinding its way upward through the hull, slowing the boat's descent until it could slide no more. The outcrop halted any further movement of the Ark within the mudslide, and so it remains embedded at its present location.

Some samples collected at the site are approximately 90% iron oxide. This evidence suggests that the metal detected *is in fact* iron. The grid of metal lines demands that the site contains a *man-made* structure and the shape is clearly that of a boat. Fasold, using a piece of high technology equipment known as *subsurface interface radar*, obtained a three-dimensional image of the underground structure.

This image revealed a measurement of the structure consistent with the Biblical dimensions of the Ark. The depth of the structure matched the measurement of 30 cubits (52 feet using the Egyptian cubit of 20.8 inches) given by God to Noah. The length and width (splayed) of the boat are in agreement with the measurements recorded by Moses in the book of Genesis; approximately 520 feet by 86 feet. (Genesis 6:15)

The cross beams were determined to be spaced every 9 feet to center. The radar also revealed rooms and 3 tiers or stories to the structure. A very interesting artifact found on the site reveals a piece of petrified wood with a spike or pin through it. On one side of the piece is a washer and there's a round head on the pin —clearly an ancient rivet. A piece of fossilized animal antler was taken from the inside of the boat, pulled out through a hole drilled into the side of the structure. Fossilized animal dung was also recovered. Wyatt had a piece of petrified wood taken off the deck of the boat. It was soon thereafter shown on CNN news in 1991.

In the immediate area, scattered on the face of the land, miles from any body of water, are at least 13 anchor stones. An anchor stone is simply an ancient anchor made of stone, with a hole in the center at the top of it, by which it was hung from the side of a ship using a length of very heavy rope. The size of each of these stones is approximately 8 feet tall by 3 feet wide by 14 inches thick, and the average weight is 8700 pounds. These stones, used by ancient ships, were lowered into the water to stabilize the ships in heavy seas, not to stop the ships from moving. Similar stones have been found on the floor of the Mediterranean and other seas.

These particular stones found in the vicinity of the Ark have petroglyphs on them, which depict the flood in many ways. Some have eight crosses on them (symbols of Noah and his family), indicating that early Christians may have revered them as memorials of the flood. The crosses are Byzantine, which indicate a time period after 300 AD. One stone bears the symbol of Nimrod, the builder of the tower of Babel, which event took place some 200 years after the flood (around 2200 BC). Other inscriptions indicate that Knights of the First Crusade may have visited the area.

There is a small village nearby, *still known* as the 'village of the eight.' In front of an ancient house there were two tombstones. Carved into the stones are a rainbow and eight symbols of Noah and his family, above an ancient petroglyphic portrayal of Noah's death on one marker, and that of his wife on the other. The graves were found looted shortly after their discovery. A very large piece of petrified wood was also found in the area and is believed to be a portion of the covering of the Ark, which Noah removed after the Ark came to rest.

A visitor's center was opened at the site by the Turkish government in 1989, however, political corruption and current unrest in the area has made travel to the site very difficult. Further excavation has not been possible to this date.[1] The discovery of Noah's Ark is one of the most important archaeological finds of all time and is a testimony to the trustworthiness of the Bible. There have been many other discoveries that also serve to bear up this trustworthiness. Unfortunately, many people remain blind and refuse to accept the reality of these things, pride being their foremost deceiver.

(Please note the pictures on page 17 of the ark, the Turkish Visitor's Center, the lines of metal detection followed and taped by David Fasold, and the photograph of one of the many anchor stones found in the area...)

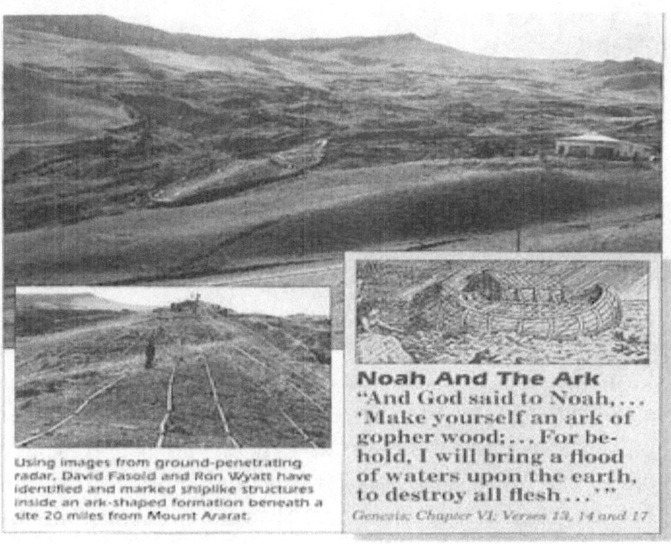

Using images from ground-penetrating radar, David Fasold and Ron Wyatt have identified and marked shiplike structures inside an ark-shaped formation beneath a site 20 miles from Mount Ararat.

*

Sodom & Gomorrah

Add to your knowledge: The fate of Sodom, Gomorrah and the cities of the plain from Genesis 19, rained upon by fire and brimstone, is no fairy tale. It was an historical event that occurred exactly as the Biblical account presents it. The remains of two of these cities can be seen on the southwestern side of the Dead Sea, just below Masada.

There are no roads into the affected areas and walking through the ash is difficult, but well worth the trek. Numerous ashen formations amid tons of ash containing embedded sulfur balls and scattered salt formations are all that remain of these cities that were destroyed by fire and brimstone (sulfur) from heaven (Genesis 19:12-29). There are ashen remains of a variety of towers, sphinxes, buildings and city walls. It is an incredibly revealing site for the believer and truth seeker.

From testing the sulfur in this area it is estimated that these cities burned at temperatures well above 4000 degrees Fahrenheit. Temperatures in this range would vaporize gold and melt stone. There is no sand or dirt at these sites, but only ash— right down to the bedrock. There are sulfur balls of various sizes throughout these ashen remains. Brimstone, or sulfur, found at these sites is contained in round pellets, some the size of golf balls. Many have been tested and are found to be 95.7% sulfur. Their round shape indicates beyond doubt that they passed through the atmosphere.

Lab tests have confirmed that the *quality* of the sulfur found in this particular area is unprecedented in the world. Some secular scientists have pointed out however that sulfur evaporates at a lower temperature than stone, such as marble, and therefore do not understand how sulfur balls could remain intact at this site...

In reply, it is obvious that sulfur balls continued to rain down upon the ashed cities after its initial super-hot firestorm burned everything up. These sulfur balls embedded themselves into the initial layers of soft ash and were cut off from oxygen. A resulting chemical reaction formed capsules around them, allowing them to be preserved in the ashen layers. Tests on the ash itself confirm it to be sulfuric ash, actually heavier than the material it replaced. Rain, wind and erosion have very little effect on this type of ash.[2]

Unique salt formations have been observed in the area of these ashen remains. The Bible says that, as Lot's wife fled from Sodom, she looked back on the destruction and was turned into a pillar of salt (Genesis 19:26). Josephus, a 1st century historian (mentioned earlier), claims to have seen her remains, as did Clement of Rome and Irenaeus in the 2nd century. There are additional eroded salt formations in the area described by Josephus that remain to this day—were others who fled perhaps turned into salt? Considering the *context* of the Biblical narration I would assume that there very well might have been.

At one time, according to Scripture, the vast area of plains upon which these cities were constructed was well watered and bore much fruit, like the Garden of Eden (Genesis 13:10). But today those cities and gardens are but ashen remains. The Bible tells us that this area would continue to bare witness as an *example* of the judgment of God upon human depravity—and so it has (2nd Peter 2:6).

An interesting note however—Jewish tour guides, who work at the ruins of Masada, high above these ash formations, refuse to accept the idea that the remains below them are those of Sodom and Gomorrah.[3] Their attitude is of course typical of those who are without knowledge concerning the works of God. Unfortunately, their ignorance is passed on to all who visit Masada—most people assume that 'tour guides' know everything.

Consider, if you will, what tour guides and even many geologists teach about the Grand Canyon, about Yellowstone and all other such wondrous places. They have very little knowledge concerning the truth about these places, especially when it comes to describing the age of something or how it was initially formed. A lack of credible knowledge in the things of God is one's worst enemy, and will eventually destroy him/her. Note also that a misunderstanding of origins has a disastrous effect upon all of the 'sciences.'

*

The Red Sea Crossing

Add to your knowledge: The location where the children of Israel crossed the Red Sea under the leadership of Moses is found on the Gulf of Aqaba, Saudi Arabia, *not* on the Gulf of Suez nor its lakes to the north, where many misinformed scholars suppose that it took place. At the Gulf of Aqaba location (Nuweiba) there is an underwater land bridge, where parts of coral covered human and animal (horse) skeletons have been retrieved. Several coral covered chariot wheels, axles and chariot boxes of Egyptian construction have also been found.

The underwater land bridge is the only one of its kind within the Red Sea, which confirms the Biblical account of the "dry ground" or "path" in the midst of the walls of sea water that God provided, allowing the children of Israel to escape from the pursuing Egyptians. The prophet Isaiah called it "the road," which God had made in the sea for the redeemed to cross over (Isaiah 51:10). This path is also mentioned in Psalm 77:19. The very existence of it is in itself a clear explanation for how the Israelites could have crossed over on "dry ground" amidst walls of water on either side.

The Israelite people had camped on the west side of the gulf just prior to crossing the sea at this point. This particular area

20

where the land bridge is located is the only area of land along the entire Gulf of Aqaba large enough to support the 1-2 million people of the Exodus. A mountain range borders this land area, Migdol (*fortification*), overlooking the sea, which is impassable to the west.

The Israelites came south into this area via a passage to the north. This entire geography is described in detail in Exodus 14:1-4. The Egyptians could have therefore only pursued them from one direction, which helped in providing the Israelites protection and escape (Exodus 14:19,20). 500 years after the actual crossing of the Red Sea, King Solomon erected two stone pillars, one on either side of the sea, to commemorate this crossing site.

These two matching pillars were found across from one another at the site of this path in the sea. Inscriptions still visible on one of them indicate that King Solomon had placed them there. The one on the Saudi side (with the inscriptions) has been removed since its discovery, probably by thieves of ancient artifacts. A marker has replaced it. The pillar on the Egyptian side is still standing, near Nuweiba, but any inscriptions have weathered away over time. Powerful storms are more frequent on that side of the Gulf.[4]

*

The Real Mt. Sinai

Add to your knowledge: Thousands visit the traditional Mt. Sinai in the southern Sinai Peninsula each year. Unfortunately for them, it is not really the Mt. Sinai of the Bible. The Bible *clearly* tells us that Mt. Sinai is in Arabia (Galatians 4:25), and so it is—standing statuesque above a broad desert plateau, a mystifying relic of antiquity in a land the Bible calls Midian, east of the Gulf of Aqaba.

The real Mt. Sinai is Jubal al Lawz (*mountain of the law*). The first thing one notices upon approaching Jubal al Lawz is its startlingly visible and mysteriously blackened peak. On the summit of the mountain, the dirt and rocks are burnt into a black and shiny marble glaze from the fire of God described in Exodus 19:16-19. These rocks atop the mountain can be broken in half, revealing an inner core of plain, brown granite—clearly not of volcanic origin.

On its craggy slopes are a mind-boggling array of ancient man-made structures and tantalizing geologic formations that come *right out of the pages of Holy Scripture*. There is a sprawling plain at the base of the mountain that would have provided an ample campsite for the Hebrew people, a primary feature missing from the area of the 'traditional' Mt. Sinai at St. Catherine's Monastery.

Near the base of the mountain, a quarter mile into the plain, there is a huge altar of stacked granite. Etched onto the altar are distinct shapes of cows and bulls, resembling the Egyptian Hathor and Apis bull gods. Cattle have never been a domesticated livestock in Saudi Arabia. The cattle memorialized in stone here were driven there by the Israelites at the time of Moses. This is the site where Aaron, Moses' brother, formed a golden calf from molten gold and made offerings on the altar, proclaiming, "Oh Israel, these are the gods who brought you out of Egypt" (Exodus 32:1-5).

At the very base of the mountain there are orderly piles of stone markers, arranged at four-hundred-yard intervals in a perfect semicircle about the mountain. These are referred to in Exodus 19:12, where the Lord ordered Moses to put *boundary* lines around the mountain so that the people would not go near the mountain, beyond the markers, where they would be put to death. Seeing is believing—these evidences speak for themselves and generate more than just awe. I have seen them, and I know.

At still another point at the foot of the mountain is a huge, V-shaped altar, clearly man-made. This was an altar of worship, built by Moses to include twelve stone pillars that represented the twelve tribes of Israel. To this day, twelve hand-hewn stumps remain there, the pillars themselves toppled over and broken into sections of which the majority still lay in disarray near the altar.

In recent years this entire region has been fenced off as a restricted archaeological site. Posted 'no trespassing' signs in both English and Arabic threaten the death penalty for any violations of the order.[5] This is of course Satan's work, hiding the truth from the world through the hearts of men. This is indeed sad, yet far worse than that is the darkness that surrounds the hearts of so-called 'believers' who don't actually believe in *any* of these evidences that I am presenting to you within this chapter.

Some of these unbelieving 'believers' have been educated by the world's collegiate system and are even referred to as *Biblical scholars*. However, they ignorantly refuse to accept the realities of God's truth, even when the facts and evidences are combined right before their eyes. Their pride and irreverence dominate our educational systems worldwide. You and your children are the victims of their madness and folly. I was fortunate—I learned more from my mother regarding the things of God, who died when I was just 14, than I did in all the years that I attended college.

*

Water from the rock at Horeb

Add to your knowledge: If you are not familiar with the rock at Horeb (*drought* or *desert*), it is located on the approach to the rocky western slopes of Sinai (the true Sinai) in a camp called Rephidim (Exodus 17:1). This was the rock that Moses struck with his staff to fulfill the promise that God would provide water in that parched, desert wasteland for the 1-2 million people of the Exodus. The split rock is indeed there, along with the evidence that the rock itself erupted like a great geyser, creating deep furrows of water erosion that are still visible to this day.

The rock sits in a shallow depression at the mouth of a ravine. It is a towering pillar of rock, split laser-fine down the middle, the split approximately nineteen inches wide from top to bottom. Its appearance alone is indeed a wonder, but the rock's inconceivable location at the crown of an ancient head-water is most impressive! It appears as if the riverbed indeed sprang from the rock itself. There are water polished boulders in this natural stream bed that runs down from the split rock; an ancient watershed furnishing clear evidence of a fast-rushing stream, indeed large enough to serve the Hebrew multitude.

While enroute to this rock at Horeb (Mt. Sinai in Arabia), the Israelites camped at a place called Elim (*terebinths*). The Bible states that there were 12 wells of water and 70 palm trees located at that particular campsite (Exodus 15:27). The 12 wells and numerous palm trees are still there in that remote area to this day.[6] This oasis is only a few days walk from Jubal al Lawz (Mt. Sinai), exactly where the Bible says it should be. What more can I say? Again, the trustworthiness of the Bible is indeed enlightening, to say the very least. Again, these evidences provide great encouragement to believers of the truth.

*

The Ark of the Covenant

Most of us have heard of the *Ark of the Covenant*. Remember Indiana Jones? Jones was the fictional archaeologist of the blockbuster movie, 'Raiders of the Lost Ark'. He indeed seemed to be the type of man we would want to employ to locate the Ark. His character and adventures have inspired many into new and renewed interest in Biblical artifacts, and that's a good thing, because they are the only *truly valuable* artifacts of any type. Add to your knowledge:

The discovery of Biblical artifacts is now on the increase.

Ancient cities mentioned in the Bible, once believed to be non-existent by skeptical critics, have more recently been unearthed. Add to your knowledge: The true Ark of the Covenant was discovered in 1982, before Indiana Jones ever came into existence on the screen. Very few people have known about the actual discovery of the Ark, due to the nature (Satan's rule) and corruption of the unbelieving world in which we live.

The Ark was thought to have been carried away from Jerusalem sometime around 587 BC, when the city fell to King Nebuchadnezzar of Babylon. But, it was not carried away. It was in fact hidden in a cave, with other temple furniture, perhaps under the direction of Jeremiah the prophet. This cave, or 'room,' was part of an ancient stone quarry, later called *Jeremiah's Grotto*. The cave is located beneath the actual Calvary escarpment, *the place of the skull*, on Mt. Moriah in Jerusalem.

A little history: The Ark of the Covenant was the only piece of furniture within a back room of the *original* Hebrew Tabernacle, or tent of meeting. This room was separated from the front room by a curtain or veil and known as the *Holy of Holies*. The front room pieces of furniture included the *altar of incense*, the *seven-lamp candlestick*, and the *table of shewbread*. The Ark (within the Holy of Holies) was a wooden chest, overlaid with gold, and at one time contained the Ten Commandments on stone, a pot of manna that never spoiled, and Aaron's rod, which once had budded miraculously overnight.

The top of this Ark was called the *Mercy Seat*, which was a flat portion between two golden cherubim that overlooked it. The High Priest alone could enter inside the Holy of Holies only *once* each year to make an annual sin offering for himself and for the people. Here, the blood of animals was sprinkled onto the *Mercy Seat* as an atonement for sin. This information regarding the atonement is indeed important for you to understand as I attempt to explain to you the location of the Ark, as well as the significance of its discovery *within* that particular location.

Keep in mind now that the Ark was hidden in a cave or chamber that existed in Jerusalem about 587 BC. In that year or near about the city was completely destroyed and its inhabitants hastened away into captivity. That the invading armies *did not discover* the whereabouts of the Ark is indicated by the fact that it is *not mentioned* in the list of treasures that had been broken and carried off by the Babylonians (2nd Kings 25:13-17, Jeremiah 52:12-23).

The table of shewbread, altar of incense and the seven-lamp candlestick are also *not among those mentioned* in the list of articles captured. The Holy Spirit inspired these Scriptures, which detail the list of treasures carried off; therefore the accuracy of that list is unquestionable. Now, gather together the mental paints and brushes in your mind and create a picture of what I am about to relate to you; as I relate it:

The city (Jerusalem) has been rebuilt upon several times since the destruction of 587 BC, each time *over top* of the previous ruins. In 1979, an excavation began atop previous ruins at the Calvary escarpment (place of the skull) or Golgotha, where Christ was crucified. No known excavations had ever taken place in this particular area since the crucifixion. The traditional site is *not* located here, where some believe it should be. This particular location was actually being used as a dump. That is so typical of men who are ignorant of God's truth. Forgetfulness of God over time plays a major part in that ignorance.

An old friend of truth and Biblical archaeology, Ron Wyatt, headed the 1979 excavation, which was one of many projects he was involved with at that time, and on through to 1989.[7] Excavating tens of feet down (below ground level) from what he believed to be the approximate site of Calvary, his team discovered the walls of a small structure surrounding what he believed to be the original crucifixion site. This building (structure) was apparently constructed during the first century to memorialize the location.

Within this structure, in the center of the rock floor, there were four cross-holes. Three were in parallel, a fourth was found under a small stone covering, elevated somewhat behind and centered on the other three. Black spots, later positively identified scientifically as human yet *unusual* bloodstains, were found near this elevated cross-hole; in a crack in the bedrock floor, underneath the small stone covering.

A *large* round seal stone (used for sealing ancient tombs) was also found within the room, lying flat on the floor, just a short distance in front of the cross-holes. This stone is now believed to be the one rolled in front of Christ's nearby garden tomb. It appeared to be memorialized here as well. Note: The nearby tomb is not the *traditional* site of the Garden Tomb, yet evidence indicates the site as authentic—a garden with a tomb in it, near the actual cross site (John 19:41).

This evidence includes physical identification of the hand-hewn track in which the stone was placed and rolled in front of the tomb, and also evidence that the tomb was sealed with a *Roman* seal, indicated by the location of unique impressions on the stone wall of the entrance on either side of the opening. That a round stone for sealing the tomb was not found *here*, but instead discovered nearby within the walls constructed around the cross-holes, is significant in determining that it must have been considered sacred by early Christians.

Over a period of time the Wyatt team's excavations continued below this room. In 1982, they discovered another room or chamber, some 20 feet below the cross-holes. Though a difficult work, Wyatt was able to make his way into this chamber, through a small but negotiable opening in the rock. His ability to move about in the chamber was hindered, due to numerous large rocks and debris that filled its interior.

He would later come to understand that an earthquake had nearly buried this chamber in rubble, yet he was destined to find some items that had been shielded from the damage caused by that eruption. In this chamber, just under a layer of large rocks, some dry rotted timbers were observed. Under the timbers, Wyatt found the dry rotted remains of animal skins. He discovered that the animal skins were covering a gold veneered table, which had a raised molding around the side, consisting of an alternating pattern of a bell and a pomegranate.

This table had the *appearance* of an object described in the original Tabernacle and used in the Temple of Solomon; the *table of shewbread*. Later, what appeared to be a golden *alter of incense* and a *seven-lamp candlestick* were identified within the chamber, covered and protected in the same manner.

Other objects were also observed, some of which appeared to be related to the original Tabernacle furniture. The greatest find was a large stone case (or chest) to the rear of the chamber. It had a flat stone covering on top, which was found to contain several cracks, and had, at some point in time, split into two separate pieces. The smaller section of the stone covering had been somehow moved aside, creating a visible opening into the interior of the stone case.

Black spots were scattered on the top of the stone covering. Samples of these 'spots' were later scientifically identified as *bloodstains*, of the same type found at the cross-hole. Immediately above the stone case there was a crack in the rock ceiling, obviously caused by an earthquake. This crack in the rock was directly above the open lid on the stone case.

Beneath the opening and inside the stone case was what appeared to be the golden *Ark of the Covenant*. Black spots of the same type found on the stone covering were observed atop what appeared to be the *Mercy Seat* of the Ark, between two golden cherubim. Ron Wyatt, Biblically informed and excited by what these discoveries might reveal, carefully fed a tape measure up into the crack in the ceiling just above the ark, and pushed it up along a crevice, running through some 20 feet of solid rock.

The end of the tape eventually appeared within the *elevated cross-hole* in the room above, and was pulled up by an utterly amazed member of the research crew. Ron Wyatt later told me that he passed out at that time—he said it was hard for him to breathe. He regained consciousness some 45 minutes later. His most *overwhelming* realization regarding this entire discovery is summarized as follows:

(a) As Christ hung on the cross there was a great earthquake, just at the time of His death. (b) Sometime later, a Roman soldier thrust a spear into Jesus' side as he hung on the cross, and His blood was shed for the remission of our sins, fulfilling Old Testament prophecy.

(c) His blood then ran down from His pierced body, onto the base of the cross, into the recently cracked rock, and followed a crevice some 20 feet down into the hidden chamber. The blood splashed onto the broken covering atop the stone case, assumed to have broken during the earthquake, where it spattered inside the opening and onto the *Mercy Seat* of the one, true *Ark of the Covenant*; thereby fulfilling forever the Old Testament law regarding the sin offering (Matthew 27:50-52, John 19:34, Hebrews 9:22,23, Leviticus 16:14-17).

Wyatt concluded, as any reasonable man would, that 600 years before Christ would die, God arranged to have His earthly throne, *the Ark with its Mercy Seat*, hidden deep within the earth, just below where His Son would die on the cross. Upon this *Mercy Seat* Christ's blood would fall, acknowledging the claims of God's *eternal* Law. The prophetical presenting of Christ's blood to His Father was *perfectly* fulfilled; no human hands presented the blood offering, and no one was in the room save the Spirit of Christ, the true High Priest.

In the earthly service, as I mentioned earlier, the Jewish High Priest offered the blood atonement once each year, sprinkling it privately onto the Mercy Seat. This was according to the Law of Moses, a foreshadowing of what was to come. Hundreds of years then passed. Christ, the true *High Priest*, was now dead—slain on the cross—His body later pierced by the spear of a Roman soldier. Yet, His Father had arranged that, even in His death, Christ would 'sprinkle' the required blood—the blood of the lamb slain from the foundation of the world—upon the *Mercy Seat*.

I was told that Wyatt at the time of that first encounter was only able to see the top portion of the Ark—the two cherubim and the Mercy Seat. He had taken several photographs of the Ark from a position near the small chamber opening, but when developed, the entire group of photos came out blurred. I have examined *one* of these photographs—the best one. The blurred image *appears* to be the top of the Ark, as described in Exodus 25:17-21. For some unknown reason the photographs are currently not available to the public.

I believe a corrupt influence is presiding at this time, which may be according to God's purpose. Ron Wyatt passed away in 1999. Informed archaeologists were afterward unable to locate the hidden chamber that he had described in his notes and drawings. Some deeper areas within the excavation had collapsed. Recent excavations as late as 2006 have still not located the hidden chamber, yet, other artifacts of 1st century Roman origin have been recovered.

The chamber containing the cross-holes within its center has been located and excavations in that area have increased. 2006 is currently the last date that information has been made available on the progress of that work. Artifacts dating back to the time of King Solomon have been unearthed. These artifacts, found below the 1st century level (Roman era), would indicate to me that they are part of a cherished collection, placed their by

Jeremiah around 587 BC, which helps to validate Ron Wyatt's theory and discovery.

The stone tablets, upon which the Ten Commandments were written by the finger of God, are believed to still be within the Ark itself, in the yet undiscovered chamber that Ron Wyatt made his way into. But due to bureaucracy, political corruption, greed, violent unrest in the area and other *providential* happenings, including mysterious and untimely deaths, these ancient Temple treasures remain unearthed to this day, well guarded amid the broken rock walls of their underground tomb.

There are those who believe that God does not at this time want the contents of the underground chamber further revealed. But, *who can know the mind of God?* (1st Corinthians 2:15,16) However, there are a few others who believe that eventually this tomb will be completely excavated, and that the whole world will be able to physically see this profound evidence. Unfortunately, in my opinion, I don't think any revelation from this excavation is going to matter to the majority of the world...

They don't care about the ark of Noah, which is sitting right out in the open—in plain sight, nor do they recognize the real Mt. Sinai and other discoveries related to it, even though several books have been written about them, explorers have visited the sites, and indisputable evidence has been presented. So, I ask you, why should they show any concern about the Ark of the Covenant and its whereabouts?

Why have all of these particularly profound Biblical archaeological discoveries, and many more throughout the earth, remained 'silent' to the majority of the world? *Why* hasn't more of the world reacted positively at the present time? The late Ron Wyatt was an exceptional man and we owe him an unprecedented respect for his supreme contribution to God's children. These discoveries are indeed *unquestionable proof* regarding the accurate testimony of God's only written word, the Bible.

As I mentioned earlier, Ron Wyatt died in 1999. David Fasold has embarked on that journey as well. Both men have since been betrayed by the world they knew—their very own people.[8] Betrayal is not uncommon among men—or among 'beings' of greater honor. God was betrayed, also by His very own; the angels who rebelled. His Son, who later came to earth, was betrayed by his own as well, those who were his closest of followers.

Satan never sleeps, yet the world seems always to be asleep. Where is everybody? Where are their minds? Why are they so stubborn in their unbelief—and why are there many professed Christians who doubt these profound evidences as well? What's it going to take to awaken people out of their sleep—out of their hardness of heart?

Jesus gave His *true* followers this answer: *The secret of the kingdom of God has been given to you. But to those on the outside everything is said in parables so that, they may be ever seeing but never perceiving, and ever hearing but never understanding; otherwise they might turn and be forgiven* (Mark 4:10-12 NIV).

This simply means that the *true followers* of Jesus will see and understand the evidences of His truth. Those who do not follow Him in *truth*, as well as those professed Christians who are actually of the world, will be spiritually blind to the truth and not be allowed to perceive it. Though the truth may be right in front of them they will not be able to see it, nor will they be able to understand it, nor will they be able to comprehend the significance of it.

God has blinded them to truth because they refuse to accept truth. He allows them to have what they love, which is the love of that which is *not* truth (Romans 1:28). This is because, in their heart of hearts, which only God can see, they truly just don't care about it. They don't really want it. It's not important to them. The sin nature has hardened them against it.

This is, sadly, the unfortunate condition of a vast majority in our world today. There are many professed Christians within this majority. The world's interest is not centered on the things of God. *The heart is deceitful above all things, and desperately wicked: who can know it?* (Jeremiah 17:9 KJV) And among Christians, Satan is out there to deceive, if possible, even the very elect (Mark 13:22). Beware! You don't know the power of the dark side.

*Note: I've rather recently been informed that early in 2007, the crucifixion excavation site and the immediate area where the Ark of the Covenant is hidden were completely cemented over by those who are now the 'governing authority' in the region. (Further information on Ron Wyatt's discoveries and the Ron Wyatt Museum can currently be found via the internet.)

*

Summary

You've been allowed a look at some profound physical evidences regarding the historical teachings of the Bible. Archaeology continues to produce overwhelming evidences as to the trustworthiness of its contents. The Bible is in fact a divinely inspired, written compass, which truly points the way, yet the creation is a living, breathing compass, which profoundly glorifies the journey. It is literally impossible for a human being to not know that God exists. We are 'without excuse' if we fail to see Him through the great wonder of the things He has made (Romans 1:20).

Let us, in respect to that principle, move on to chapter 2 and take a closeup look at the physical earth itself—a look at the evidence it can offer to your learning. At this time you might want to take a hike into a wilderness area and park yourself on a rock, perhaps down by a stream, to truly appreciate your reading of this most informative upcoming chapter...

Chapter Two:

A Look at the Earth

The main reason that I requested you read this book while relaxing in the wilderness is because there are some things you'll need to understand about the landscape itself. With a deeper understanding of the landscape, it becomes much easier to see God's hand in it—to take special notice of some things that you may have not actually noticed before. You may be one to believe that God formed all of the great wonders around us, or you may not be one who believes...

Add to your knowledge: Sir Isaac Newton is most famous for the discovery of gravity, but he also formulated the three laws of universal motion and helped to develop the math known as calculus. His work laid the foundation for the great scientific law of energy conservation, and he developed the particle theory of light propagation. As an astronomer, he made the first reflecting telescope.

Newton, a believer in the Creator, wrote papers defending creation and the Bible. He believed that the worldwide flood, as described in Genesis, accounted for most of earth's features. He also believed in the six-day creation account found in Genesis. Newton said, "This most beautiful system of the sun, planets and comets could only proceed from the counsel and dominion of an intelligent and powerful being."

What you learned in high school and college regarding the origin of the earth and its landscape were the theories and presumptions of secularly educated men and women—human beings like yourself. School textbooks today are full of errors on this subject. As a matter of fact thousands of error-filled books have been written regarding the earth and its neighboring planets —the entire solar system as well. This is Satan's domain (Luke 4:5-6, 1st John 5:19). He will hide the truth from you personally through a great variety of deceptions as long as you allow him to do that.

Add to your knowledge: It's time to learn what *really* took place and to gain a better understanding of what you are looking at. God created the earth, the solar system, and the myriad of operations or actions that sustain/uphold them. Therefore, He is the only one who can tell you the absolute truth about it all, just as He is the only one who can help you to know and understand just who you are as a person, and what your purpose is here on the earth—why you have been given life at this particular point in time.

John Woodward lived from 1665-1728, and was one of the first paleontologists—scientists who study fossils. He believed the fossil record showed great evidence for the worldwide flood of the Bible. Samuel F. B. Morse is best known for his invention of the telegraph. He also designed the first camera in America. Morse once wrote:

"The nearer I approach to the end of my pilgrimage, the clearer is the evidence of the divine origin of the Bible, the grandeur and sublimity of God's remedies for fallen man are more appreciated, and the future is illuminated with hope and joy."

As I have stated earlier, the Bible is a divinely inspired, written compass, which truly points the way, but the creation is a living, breathing compass, which profoundly glorifies the journey. It is impossible for a human being to not know that God exists. We are 'without excuse' if we fail to see Him in and through the wonder of the things He has made (Romans 1:20).

Having an authentic understanding of the earth and all that you see around you is a knowledge that allows you to be quite special. Not everyone will come to understand what you are about to learn. Once you have a more authentic understanding of what you see out there, it can bring great comfort in times of personal failure, despair, loneliness, fear, doubt, anxiety, affliction, pain and suffering, and anything else of this likeness that the wind might blow your way.

I'm a hiker by nature. I spend much time in the wilderness. Mountains, deserts, forests, you name it—been there and done that, and I am still doing it. That's my world—the world I've come to know, which is a very peaceful one. The wilderness offers much inspiration and encouragement. It's uniquely informative as well. Again, the Bible teaches us that we can know that God exists through the things he has made. The utter depth of that statement is unfathomable.

To see the creativity of God in each of His wonders—from a simple blade of grass to a flower, a bush, a tree, a grain of sand, a pebble, a stone, a rock, a high mountain, lush fields, desert plains, mountain streams, lakes and whatever else the eyes can take in, is a great privilege. To reach out and touch any of these wonders is indeed an honor. The Master Creator's work is unequaled.

The glory of a sunrise and the sunset, the vast array of stars in the night sky and the phases of the moon have for centuries given inspiration and hope to many people throughout the world. God created these wonders for the education and pleasure of mankind. The depth of love behind all of this is for sure incomprehensible.

When I am hiking along on a trail I am at times

overwhelmed with the undeserved satisfaction of being allowed to view such things. God pours out His love before me. When I hear the pebbles pushed aside under my hiking boots with each step, I am in awe of the sound that they make. There are also the sounds of the wind and the rain, the animals and the birds—even the insects and the crawling things have distinct sounds of their own. I am also able to sense the quality of silence in such a place, to smell the air and to feel the heat or the cold.

I realize that I am fearfully and wonderfully made as a human being (Psalm 139:14), and I am at a loss to understand the grand architecture involved in my makeup. How wondrous is this thing called life! Absolute love was indeed at the center of all things created. I am most fortunate to have learned just who I am and what I am all about. This knowledge is great power for living life in a fallen world.

I am fortunate also to have been allowed to now share this knowledge with you. If you are reading this book then you have become my assignment, so to speak. I pray that you will not be disappointed. Educating body, mind and spirit is a good thing for you, and will allow you to live free—no longer a slave to the world of sin and corruption in which you were born. That's true freedom—indeed the only real freedom there is.

It's time for you to get truly educated regarding the landscape upon which you live. As I mentioned earlier, knowing these things will allow you a special knowledge that can give you much strength when you need it, in addition to some profound wisdom. It was by wisdom that all created things were formed (Proverbs 8:22-31). Whoever finds wisdom finds life, and obtains favor from the Lord. Whoever hates (rejects) wisdom is said to love death (Proverbs 8:35, 36).

And by the way, for all of you ladies out there, the 'Spirit of Wisdom' is female in nature (Proverbs 8:1-4). I find that rather exciting. No, in spite of popular opinion, it's not just a man's world out there. It's my belief that the Godhead is made up of male and female personalities—the 'first family of heaven', if you will. It only makes sense.

Most scientific dating techniques today indicate that the earth and solar system are very young—possibly less than 10,000 years old. My own calculations are somewhere between 6000 to 7000 years old, and a host of well-known scientists agree with those figures. One primary indication in support of this fact, among many others, is *excess fluid pressure*.

Abnormally high oil, gas and water pressures exist within relatively permeable rock all over the globe. If these fluids had been trapped more than 10,000 to as much as 100,000 years ago, leakage would have dropped these pressures *far below* what they are today. Therefore, this oil, gas, and water must have been trapped quite suddenly and recently.[1]

Personally I hold to the Biblical age of the earth, which is now just a little over 6000 years, and, as I mentioned earlier, many scientists are in agreement. We don't usually hear about the opinions of these particular scientists or get involved in studying their findings. Remember that it's Satan's domain. He is the ruler of the kingdoms in the world, and his literature and methods of education dominate the world's systems. He does not want you to learn the truth in these matters from those in the know, but here it is…

Approximately 1,656 years after the creation of the first man, God brought a catastrophic, global flood of waters upon the earth. At that time mankind's wickedness upon the earth was exceedingly great. Every imagination from the thoughts of men's hearts was only evil continually (Genesis 6:5). The population of the earth at that time is estimated to be 900,000,000 (nine hundred million), and that is a conservative estimate.[2]

In keeping with His promise to bring a Savior into the world, God determined to save just one family from the worldwide flood, who found grace in His eyes. That particular family had just eight members. The family was that of Noah (meaning *rest*), a man of integrity. Noah was not chosen for his personal integrity, but through God's grace as a type of Christ.

Noah represented his own family as Christ represents His. Noah's descendants would eventually bring the Savior into the world. The population that currently exists has descended from Noah (that means you and I also). The effects of the Great Flood are most important to us today because it helps us to better understand the geography and geology of our present earth, yet it also helps us, through recorded population studies after the Great Flood, to more accurately trace our ancestry back to Noah…

For instance, languages are related, as are human genes. One of thousands of examples is the word for "from" or "of". It exists in French (*de*), Italian (*di*), Spanish (*de*), Portuguese (*de*), and Romanian (*de*). These languages, now spoken generally in southwestern Europe, are twigs on a tree branch called the Romance languages (Romance meaning *Rome*).

This branch joins a larger branch that includes all languages derived primarily from Latin. They merge with other large branches, such as the Germanic branch that includes English, into a family called the Indo-European languages. When these and other languages are traced back in time, they converge near the Mountains of Ararat, the landing site of Noah's Ark.[3]

However, most importantly, knowledge of what the Great Flood has *produced* allows us to see God in His creation—His attributes—with indeed much clarity. By continuing your journey through this writing your eyes will be opened to the unfathomable love of God, if they haven't been already.

This love, which passes understanding, can convince the most rebellious in heart of their need to learn to love Him in return. It can break the most stubborn will or serve to heal the loneliest among the brokenhearted, downtrodden or afflicted.

What person would not want eternal life, if all things in this present world could be made new—if he/she could start life all over in a perfect world? How would you like all of your dreams to come true? I hope you'll continue this hike and see for yourself what is possible. What you can discover through the creation can help motivate you to learn more about God from the pages of the Bible, His *only written revelation* to us. You can learn much more about yourself as well.

Most people are familiar with the story of Noah and the Flood. Unfortunately most are unaware of how to actually *see* the story in the earth, due to the shortsightedness in a host of modern 'scientists' and the 'educational' philosophies of the times. However, though the story is nearly 5000 years old, its evidence remains all around us (Romans 1:20). The earth tells us this profound story without wavering—without question.

You do not now see the earth that existed at the time of the Garden of Eden. It was much different in those times before the flood. The earth was perfect and complete in every detail. There were no desolate lands, no barren hills nor polar icecaps, and no scorching desert heat—no desert at all. But that perfection gradually changed after the fall in Eden, and then changed dramatically through a series of cataclysmic convulsions associated with the Great Flood.

The fossils have accelerated the imaginations of men since the time of the early Egyptians. Many later cultures have had some very unusual ideas about them as well, but in today's times of advanced archaeological and true scientific discovery the evidence becomes much clearer. The fossils offer conclusive proof that the physical conditions of the world before the flood of Noah—the climate, animals, plant life and living space—were vastly different from that of our world today. Fossils do not lie and have certainly been preserved by God for a purpose.

With respect to climate, the fossils show that there was a consistently mild climate in high and low altitudes of both the northern and southern hemispheres. That is; there was a perfectly uniform, non-zonal, mild and spring like climate in every part of the globe.

There were a far greater variety of birds and animals in the pre-flood world. As to size they ranged from the stature of a wolf to that of immense creatures over one hundred feet in length. In the Canadian province of Alberta alone twenty-six different species of the pre-flood world have been identified. Thousands of marine specimens have been found in several of our own western states, which indicate that a sea on the pre-flood earth may have covered these areas.

The pre-flood earth contained more living space for the human race than this present world offers. The world of Adam and his immediate descendants contained proportionately more habitable land. There were no enormous waste areas, such as the great deserts of Africa, Asia, America and Australia, nor were the landmasses separated by such a vast expanse of ocean water, which today constitutes over three quarters of the earth's surface. Because of such vast oceans, ice-covered continents and other barren land areas, only about one half of the land that now exists on the earth is habitable.

The earth after the flood was not only reduced considerably in land area, but the fertility of the soil and the natural resources necessary for human existence are now unequally apportioned. Because of this unbalanced distribution of land conditions the people in some areas live in plenty, while others eke out a miserable existence. This difference gives rise to envy, strife, opposition and brutal wars between the nations.

Each area of land however is not without its particular beauty and specific contribution to the whole. If all humans in all parts of the globe could focus on these more important aspects, our cultures might better relate to and cooperate with one another.

The pre-flood earth probably had only one very large super continent, covered substantially with lush vegetation (Genesis 1:9). There were seas and major rivers (Genesis 1:10 & 2:11-14). The mountains were smaller than today's, but perhaps 9000 feet high.

This is established by the fact that marine deposits of great thickness, formed in deep water, have been and are continuing to be found at elevations from 10,000 to 16,000 or more feet above the current sea level.

The fossils show also that thousands of land animals died suddenly in all parts of the world, the majority buried alive under tons of sediments. Large deposits of animal bones are found in all parts of the world. It is said that the vast arctic plain of Siberia contains so many animal bones that it is assumed that the frozen ground matter consists *entirely* of them.

Masses of fish fossils have also been preserved, caught by sediments and instantly fossilized in swimming positions— uninjured, eyes bulging and fins extended in terror. The world's dense vegetation (thick forests, plants and all other growth) was also compressed rapidly and under extreme and even unimaginable force. The great coal beds found in every continent of the earth today are the proofs concerning the density of vegetation that once existed before the flood.

Coal is simply compressed vegetable matter. It has been estimated that it requires from 10 to 14 feet of vegetable matter to produce a seam of coal just 1 foot in thickness. There are many seams of coal throughout the world ranging from 40 to 50 feet in thickness. One particular Antarctic expedition found an entire mountain of coal at the South Pole. A coal seam measuring from 60 to 90 feet in thickness was discovered in a strip mine in Wyoming. This particular large seam of coal represents a solid mass of vegetation, trees and other plants from 500 to 1000 feet in thickness.

Oil is also found in fossiliferous strata and is therefore not an original creation, but a product of organic matter. Some scientists conclude, with convincing proof, that myriads of fishes destroyed in the cataclysmic cycles of the Great Flood are the source of practically the entire supply of crude petroleum. It is also believed that animal fats are a portion of the supply as well.

A German scientist placed animal fats in a sealed container and exposed them to extreme heat and pressure. The end result of his experiment was petroleum. There are many books in print authored by a variety of scientists that can give you much more detail regarding the profound fossil evidence of the Great Flood.[4]

It becomes obvious why God, with exceeding grief, would not allow some of his larger living creatures to resume life after the flood. They were predominately vegetarians, who would no longer have the great abundance of lush vegetation available to them on the post-flood earth.

The post-flood earth is what you and I see on the landscape. If you go into the areas where there has been little human influence (no large cities, highways, or works of men) you can see the results of the flood. Though the evidence is about 5000 years old, it is still quite distinct in the mountains, valleys and canyons of the world.

In the Alabama Hills of Lone Pine, California, I began talking much about the flood on video, demonstrating the uniqueness of its aftermath and presenting it on film. Great water-carved formations abound here, and from atop Mt. Whitney you can get a most revealing aerial view of the formations that were constructed by the cataclysm, as well as the distinct floodplain that was later formed by the receding waters of the flood.

The Great Flood formed even Mt. Whitney itself and the entire range of the Sierra Nevada. Do you think the earth is beautiful now? Indeed it is, yet it is entirely the aftermath of the Great Flood—you've actually been looking at *flood damage* all of your life. I don't like to think of it as *damage*, but, considering the supremacy of the pre-flood earth, it *is* damage—yet, one can see God's hand in the entire work.

We see beautiful mountains, deserts, canyons, trees and plants and flowers of the field—myriads of varieties of beautiful things—unsurpassed in our time! But, before the process of nature allowed these things to bloom to such perfection once again, the world was indeed a barren place. The Great Flood reshaped the entire earth; moving its mountains, carving its canyons, laying down its deserts, forming its vast oceans, and cleansing it as well—of all life.

Only eight people stepped out of an ark onto a bleak earth, an earth washed clean of wickedness. They had all the animals and birds that would populate this bleakness aboard their ship! *Note*: There are those who do not believe that the Ark could have contained all the pairs of animals and birds that God chose to bring aboard it. There's evidently some misunderstanding here; the Ark had a capacity of nearly 3,600,000 cubic feet. In reality, nearly 1000 railroad boxcars could fit into a ship of this size—more than enough room for the chosen species and ample room to spare for food.

Can you focus your mind and imagine yourself to be in their place when the family of Noah first stepped out onto dry land, after residing over a year in the ark? Can you fathom yourself as one of the eight people in the entire world whom God had chosen to save? Think about this. There are places in the wilderness where you can hike and find yourself completely alone—far from the civilized world. There's no man-made noise —nothing but scenery and silence. You can actually hear an eagle in flight a long way off. You may hear a bee buzzing about a flower. Such silence is glorious. It is breathtaking!

I'm going to give you a brief overview of the physical flood itself—how it came about. However, before I go into that, there is some additional information that has been gleaned from the fossils—information that you probably won't find in your modern day science journals. Fossils teach us that mankind before the flood had not only multiplied and become a great people, but had also taken possession of the earth and had reached perhaps a higher stage of civilization and culture than we know today.

Pre-flood mankind was, in spite of their eventual fall into depravity, a much greater and more intelligent species than previously thought. They were not strictly cave dwellers who were physically deformed and didn't know how to speak, as commonly taught by modern educational institutions. Actually, it would only stand to reason that the generations before the flood had extremely more mental capacity than men of today…

Consider Adam, who named all of the birds and animals (Genesis 2:19). There is no one living today who could commit that much knowledge to memory. Adam was extremely intelligent as were his immediate descendants. The Genesis account teaches us that Adam's descendants had a considerable knowledge of mathematics, were foremost in the creation and use of tools, and had an advanced understanding in the art of building.

They were master metal craftsmen as well, and had an unequaled appreciation for gold and precious stones. They engaged in farming, industry, arts and inventions, music and poetry, and those things of life that are only found in an advanced civilization. The fossils tell us that it was actually the golden age in the history of man, of which the various mythologies of later ages are but a faint and indistinct echo.

But, there is another side to this picture, for parallel with these great material and cultural achievements there runs a steady course of moral decay and spiritual degeneracy (Genesis 6:5). Their thoughts were bent only upon doing evil continually. However, depraved as they were, they might not necessarily have been a pagan or idolatrous race.

Archaeology of grave sites found beneath the flood sediments have produced no figure of a god, or any symbol or ornament that strikes one as being of a religious nature.[5] If they were not a religious people by nature, then deductive reasoning tells me that they were intelligent enough to know that there was only one God, and that they chose to rebel against Him, which reasoning the Bible verifies as accurate.

Religious practices are a product of a lesser intelligence—of not knowing that there is only one true God, who made all things. Religious beliefs and superstition are what is produced when people choose to worship man-made gods—creations of their imaginations or handmade idols, which they foolishly consider to be sacred.

If these pre-flood people made no physical idols, then they were an idol to themselves, which explains their practice of only evil continually. They separated themselves from their Creator by choice; they did not honor God nor were they thankful, as Romans 1:21 suggests.

The great worldwide flood of Noah took place somewhere around 2460 BC. There are some who disagree with this date, but a careful study will reveal it to be quite accurate. Also, a detailed and scientific reconstruction of this event can at present be made independently of the Scriptures.

You can see on our planet seventeen or more very strange features, which can now be systematically explained as the result of a cataclysmic, global flood, whose waters erupted from subterranean chambers, with an energy release exceeding the explosion of 10 billion hydrogen bombs.

Take your time on this—concentrate on each paragraph and develop a mental picture here. This explanation will come alive for you. This explanation shows us just how rapidly major mountains were formed. It explains the widespread coal and oil deposits, and the rapid continental drift. It explains why, on the ocean floor, there are huge trenches and hundreds of canyons and volcanoes. It explains the formation of the layered strata (layers of soil and rock) and most of the fossils. It explains the frozen mammoths, the 'so-called' ice ages, and major land canyons, especially the Grand Canyon.

The Bible speaks of subterranean waters below the earth's surface (Genesis 2:6). This water conceivably amounted to about half of what is now in our oceans. This water was contained in interconnected chambers, forming a thin, spherical shell about a half a mile thick, perhaps 10 miles below the earth's surface (see fig.1).

In keeping with His promise to judge the old world and bring forth a Savior, the Spirit of God, on a chosen day, allowed the pressure in these subterranean water chambers to increase. His method of course remains unknown. This increasing pressure stretched the crust of the earth—much like a balloon stretches when the pressure inside increases.

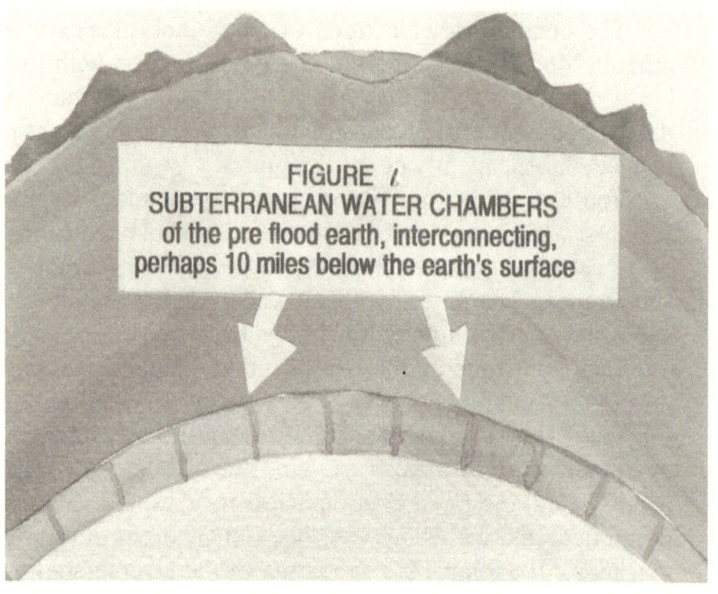

Drawings in this chapter created by *Sandra M. Eisenhower*

Failure in the crust began with a microscopic crack, which grew in both directions at about 3 miles per second. The crack, following the path of least resistance, encircled the globe in

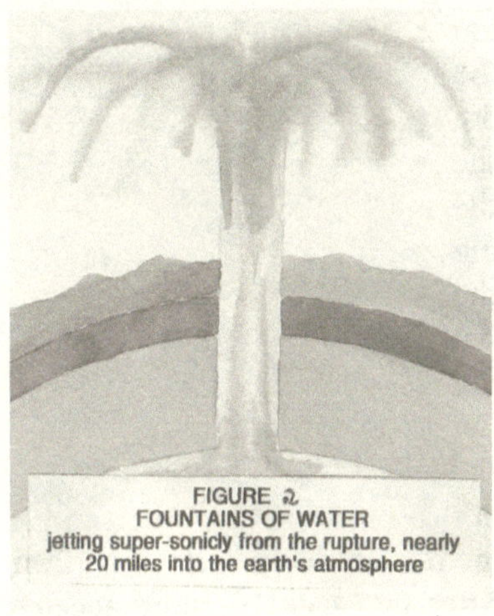

FIGURE 2
FOUNTAINS OF WATER
jetting super-sonicly from the rupture, nearly 20 miles into the earth's atmosphere

about 2 hours. As the crack raced around the earth, the overlying rock crust opened up—like a rip in a tightly stretched cloth. The subterranean water was under extreme pressure because of the weight of the 10 miles of rock pressing down on it. As the crust opened up the water then exploded violently (fig.2) out of the rupture. Along this globe encircling rupture, fountains of water jetted upward supersonically, reaching almost 20 miles into the atmosphere.

The wide spray from these enormous fountains produced torrential rains, such as the earth has never experienced before or after the flood. The Bible says that, in one day, all the fountains of the great deep were broken up and the windows of heaven were opened (Genesis 7:11).

The water jetting up from the rupture into the cold

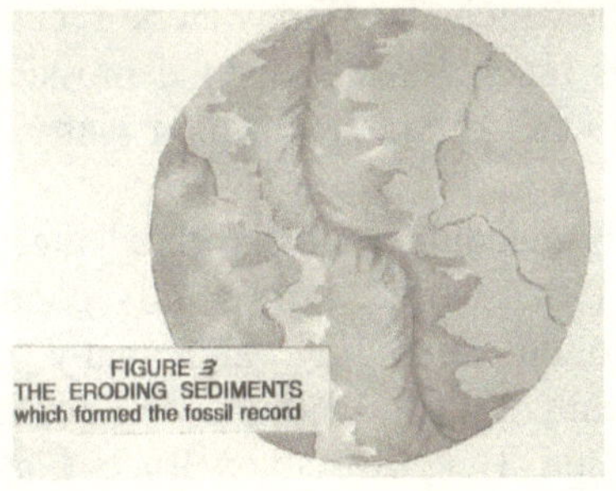

FIGURE 3
THE ERODING SEDIMENTS
which formed the fossil record

atmosphere froze into super cooled ice crystals, producing some massive ice dumps; burying, suffocating, and instantly freezing many animals, including the frozen mammoths of Siberia and Alaska. These high-pressure fountains eroded the rock on both sides of the crack, producing huge volumes of sediments that settled out of this muddy water all over the earth. The sediments trapped and buried plants and animals, both large and small, all over the earth, forming the fossil record (fig.3).

The water erosion continued to widen the rupture. Eventually the width was so great that the compressed rock beneath the subterranean chamber sprung upward, giving birth to the *mid-oceanic ridge* (fig.4) that wraps around the earth like the seam of a baseball. The continental plates (the hydroplates) still with

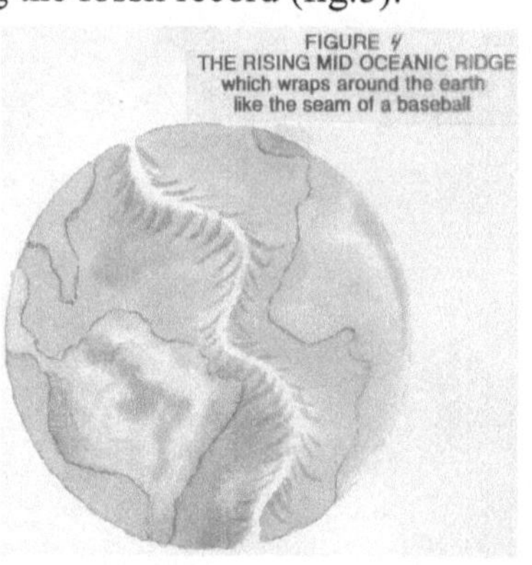

lubricating water beneath them, slid down hill away from the rising mid-oceanic ridge. After the massive, slow accelerating continental plates reached speeds of about 45 miles per hour, they ran into resistances, compressed, and then buckled.

The portions of the hydroplates that buckled downward formed ocean trenches, while those that buckled upward formed mountain ranges. This is why the major mountain chains are parallel to the oceanic ridges from which they slid. The hydroplates, in sliding away from the oceanic ridges, opened up very deep ocean basins into which the floodwaters eventually retreated. On the continents, each bowl shaped depression or basin was naturally left brim full of water, forming many post-flood lakes.[6]

The Great Flood and its receding waters formed the most beautiful hiking country in the world. Within this continent alone; Grand Canyon, Monument Valley, and many other National Parks such as Death Valley, Yellowstone, Yosemite, Grand Teton, Saguaro, Joshua Tree, Sequoia, Bryce Canyon,

Shenandoah, the Great Smokey Mountains, Kings Canyon, and many, many other unique formations all over the continent. Very special artwork comprises each of these formations. Design is also evident in the myriad of formations, both small and great, throughout the entire world.

It is important to note here, so that you might understand the scope of the Great Flood and therefore be better able to comprehend its results, that the waters of the flood were *extremely high* upon the earth. The waters prevailed at over 22 feet *above the highest mountain* for several months (Genesis 7:20). The effect of this enormous amount of water pressure on the earth's surface, which brought about such radical changes in the landscape and formed the fossil record, would, under the *normal* operation of the laws of nature, require *millions of years* to accomplish.

The water was so high when recession began that it took over five months for the newly formed mountains to become visible. During this recession, water moved with *incalculable force* over the recently deposited sediments of the flood. The rock, sand and debris in these powerful waters fine-tuned the mountains, re-shaped the landscape, opened valleys, carved immense canyons, scattered rocks and huge boulders over hundreds of miles of territory, leaving us thousands of diverse formations—formations that we see nowadays and seem to take for granted.

We are currently taught to believe that they evolved 'somehow' over millions of years and have always been here. Nothing could be further from the truth.[7] When one stands in the presence of these formations there is no 'somehow.' The mysteries of the ages unfold by merely opening your eyes to the incredibly creative power of a loving God.

You can see His strength and His gentleness. You can see His passion and His sense of humor. And what did He use to form it all? He used water, the most powerful force in nature, to cleanse the earth and give it new birth. Water is significantly essential to new birth—to salvation—to life. Nothing lives without water—that's just the Designer's way. Water is a great witness to His work.

Water saved Noah in bringing the ark to safety during the Great Flood. Water saved Moses and the Israelite Nation when the pursuing Egyptians were drowned in the Red Sea. Under the New Covenant, water also represents the cleansing of one's past sins by the word of God through the blood of Christ in baptism. (Acts 2:38, 22:16, Romans 6:3-10, Galatians 3:27, 1st Peter 3:20,21, etc.)

Again, that's the Designer's way. It is also a 'scientific' fact that nothing can come into being without water. It is scientifically true that nothing can live without water. It is an ingredient in the makeup of every living species of plant and creature on the face of the earth. Water is both a creator and sustainer of life. Water was a primary force in the initial formation of the earth, long before the Great Flood. God used inconceivable amounts of water in the creation of things—a myriad of things.[8]

The Bible warns us that we are without excuse—contrary to popular opinion we *can* know that God exists and come to understand Him through the things He has made (Romans 1:20). God strengthens us, increasing our faith in Him through this readily discernible knowledge. I sincerely hope that this chapter has allowed you to look somewhat differently at the world you live in and the earthly landscape upon which you now walk.

When you examine a rugged landscape up close there is much you can learn about God, the Artist. Unique displays of colors abound in rocks of all sizes and shapes. From the tiny pebbles under my hiking boots to the large boulders, slabs, and huge granite mountains upon which I have trod, I have found unfathomable diversity in both color and design in stone. I have seen a *quality* of love that motivates within me a compelling desire to appreciate—to love in return.

These rocks and the various granite mountains, with their impressive, lofty crags, are the rocks upon which our faith becomes tangible. They are the truths that can form the *rock of knowledge* within our hearts—a firm foundation that we can build upon, ever increasing our appreciation, our understanding, and our faith in our Creator and Friend. This is indeed a love worth finding.

It is in fact through this love and respect that we come to know and understand just who we are. Add to your knowledge: Let us at this time take a hike through some exceedingly great wonders that have been formed in our American desert...

Let me understand the teaching of Your precepts; then I will meditate on Your wonders.

Psalm 119:27

Authors Note:

Great are Your wonders, O Lord; what a living portrait of artwork they paint, and what a profoundly inspirational story they tell!

Chapter Three: **The Desert Trail**

I was fortunate to have visited the American southwest several times from 1998 to 2002. I lived in and worked from a Prowler trailer at that time, a cozy 17 footer, which I hauled around from place to place with a sturdy and dependable, slightly old Ford pick-up truck. The trailer had a most comfortable and convenient layout inside, warmly decorated with a variety of inspiring souvenirs that I had either collected or created from the wilderness areas I had been allowed to both visit and work in.

Now, it's your turn. You are about to embark on a unique journey into the deserts of the American southwest. Within these vast, spiritually captivating, rugged areas of sand, rocks, ravines and exquisite formations, you will have an opportunity to draw a privileged nourishment from the things that God has so wonderfully made. This particular nourishment can serve to greatly increase your understanding of God, as well as that of yourself. It can teach you how to love the One who loves you.

Each of us are given certain abilities and special purpose in life that we might, as individuals and together, accomplish God's will for us. The quality time you're about to spend on the Desert Trail may indeed serve to enlighten you in the relevant knowledge and comprehension of these things. All you will need on this journey is an adequate supply of drinking water, a few snacks in you backpack, a Bible, and a good hiking stick. You will need your mental camera as well. Ready? Let's do it…

God and Arches

He does great things past finding out, yes, wonders without number (Job 9:10 NKJV).

Arches National Park is quite a distinguished monument of our Creator, a garden of sculpture and one that definitely leaves you in awe over the creative power of water. God has indeed left some real images of art for us to view here. Some of them are actually humorous. Don't think for one minute that God doesn't have a sense of humor. Consider Uluru (Ayers Rock) in central Australia...

Here is one solid rock, hundreds of miles from anywhere in the middle of a flatland nowhere, some 986 feet high and over 5 miles in circumference. It's been called, "a remarkable pebble." Everyone in the world wonders how the heck this big 'pebble' ever got out there in the middle of nowhere? Don't think for one minute that God did not laugh when he planned its placement there during the convulsions of the Great Flood.

Geologists from all parts of the world speculate and converse on this wonder, hiking all over it and offering many suggestions as to the origin of its formation. God laughs, not at them, but at their foolishness of heart. They look at it, scratching their heads in wonder, while He sits in heaven and grins, hoping that they will get a grip on reality, acknowledge His creative work, and thank Him for His kindness in allowing anyone the pleasure of hiking upon it.

Our hike through Arches National Park will also confirm God's unprecedented artwork and sense of humor in a most remarkable way. The initial flood deposits in this area (about 2460 BC) consisted of a vast number of hills and mounds of good quality clay, which were, just a brief time later, reformed and finely sculptured by the divinely guided movement (operation) of receding waters.

God indeed left some profound shapes here. I call it the *check this out, folk's* display of God's handiwork. The artwork here is most impressively representative of the human race and of the present animal inhabitants of the earth. There are some Biblical students who believe that this area is the remains of an ancient city; that the sculpturing is actually the work of men. That's a possibility but not a probability.

The secular opinion of course is that Arches was eroded into these shapes by wind and water over millions of years. We know that idea is absurd; an absolute impossibility in the mind of the true Christian or the true scientist, since the earth itself, as we know it, is just over 6000 years old. The young earth explains many things that the unbelieving wrestle with and are ignorant of. Deceitfulness of the heart and the inability to reason are the culprits. Having your eyes open yet closed play a prominent role as well.

My personal opinion is that God challenges mankind here at Arches, but in a kind and humorous way. Knowing that we *should* be able to see His mind in these works here (Romans 1:18-20), knowing that He is going to have the so-called experts come up with all kinds of explanations here, and knowing thirdly that

He is going to *delight* those who have true understanding (His *own* children), He allowed that this area, later named by men as *Arches National Park*, would be a monument to the creativity of God and perhaps a preview of the eventual history of mankind in the United States of America.

Take a real close look. There are a myriad of shapes here. Of the animals there are elephants, horses, cattle, sheep and rams, lions, coyotes, and birds such as the hawk and the eagle. Of men there are the images of George Washington, Thomas Jefferson and other figures of the Revolution. There are infants in the arms of women, patriots marching and casualties of war.

Abraham Lincoln is giving an oratory at a podium. There are civil war soldiers lurking about and slaves huddled in fear. There are statues of American Indians, while on a considerably larger scale are the scar-faced profiles of Indian warriors and chiefs. There are also groups here and there which appears to be a diversity of people engaged in prayer. Then there's Park Avenue; walls of rock that resemble downtown New York City.

There is indeed much more to be found here, and it doesn't take *any* stretch of the imagination to do so. The famous *Delicate Arch*, the location of which is indeed an inspiring hike over red rock, looks like the torso and legs of a bowlegged cowboy wearing a pair of chaps. He may have been whole at one time, as there is a lot of broken rock in the valley directly below him.

In a canyon just behind this arch is a group of women standing around a well. There are huge bowls that resemble pottery here and at other locations throughout the park as well. There are rocks that resemble pueblos and still others that resemble castles. Depending on the time of day, the shadows created by the sun making its way through the park serve to highlight this grand display of artwork in a diversity of ways. Towering spires, pinnacles and balanced rocks perched atop seemingly inadequate bases are among these scenic spectacles.

Then there are the many and varied arches themselves. There are more than 2,000 arches within the park, ranging in size from a three foot opening (the minimum considered to be an arch) to the longest one, *Landscape Arch*, which measures 306 feet from base to base. Some of the arches are extremely tall, with huge spans, and you will seasonally find an occasional rock climber atop them.

I myself enjoy viewing the clouds through the archways as they pass behind, providing an excellent backdrop and continuously changing their exquisite formations. There are great photo opportunities here. I once photographed the moon during daylight hours through the span of a lengthy arch. It was indeed an impressive photo for an amateur—postcard material for sure.

After sunset many arches throughout the park provide unique views of the evening stars through their open archways. *Why* so many arches? God likes arches. He is not unlike us in having favorites; the first thing He gave us after the Great Flood was an arch. Remember the *rainbow*? It is still around—a tribute to the flood and a sign from God, confirming His promise to never again destroy the earth with water.[1]

Again, there's much to see in this unique area of land where most of this particular composition of clay, over the last 5000 years or so, has hardened to stone. All of the clay formations in the area look as if they were baked in an oven. Indeed, the sun's heat over a period of time is surely responsible for this work. Perhaps it only took a few years after the formations were born to accomplish this. Geologists have numerous theories on this particular aging process, but only God knows.

Modern geology does not take into consideration that God made all things and a variety of them full grown; therefore their conclusions on any matter regarding the aging process require a great deal of scrutiny. In other words, no disrespect intended, their intelligence is more foolishness than it is anything else.[2] All I know for sure is that the entire area of Arches National Park is a most remarkable display of His handiwork. (Psalm 95:5 & 104:8 Isaiah 40:28, Acts 7:50 & 17:24).

There's a particular arch within the park that is called Delicate Arch. I mentioned it earlier. It's about a 3 mile round trip hike over the most beautiful expanse of red rock that one can imagine. It is a well known monument, frequently pictured in travel journals. I've been allowed to hike to it several times over the years. The first time that my artist friend, Sandie, went to the Arches with me she chose to make the hike to the Delicate Arch. She has always had trouble with her ankles and I questioned her, surprised that she wanted to make the effort.

Well, she did it, living with the ankle discomfort along the way. When she finally reached the Arch she burst into tears. I asked her if she was in pain. She just shrugged her shoulders and said, "It is so beautiful—I am really glad that you let me come along." To me, her hike was a monumental accomplishment. I am sure it was to her as well. I took a photograph of her standing in front of the arch, and later decoupaged it onto wood. It is currently on display in her home office. When she on occasion allows herself to get down in the dumps with life, I just tell her to gaze in wonder and awe at that picture...

Thanks for taking the time out of your day to hike here with me through this outstanding red rock country. I hope you too were inspired! It is certainly a great place to wander through, to allow your mind to take the time to ponder the wonder of God in His unequaled creativity. It is a place to meditate deeply on all His works and to consider, within our finite minds, the infinite height and breadth of His wisdom.   *All things were made through Him, and without Him nothing was made that was made* (John 1:3 NKJV).

Monument Valley

Remember His marvelous works, which He has done, His wonders... (Psalm 105:5 NKJV).

If you've never hiked *Monument Valley*, well, it's time you did. These impressive wonders, sacred to the Navajo nation, are located in an area of about ninety-two thousand acres, which is just a small part of the nearly 16 million acre Navajo Indian Reservation of the great American southwest.

The monuments themselves are scattered across the landscape from northern Arizona into southern Utah. The elevation here is high desert country, from about 5000 to just over 6000 feet or more above sea level. The first thing you may want to take note of on your trek through this land, if and when the wondrous awe generated inside you ever settles down long enough for you to do so, is to note the *height* of the various monuments.

For the most part they are all very close to the same height above ground. The floor of the valley presently consists of small, rolling hills and flatland, mostly hardened clay and sandstone (similar to the terrain of Arches National Park). The monuments themselves are composed of a tightly compressed mixture of the terrain found at ground level.

The point is that during the Great Flood, about 5000 years ago, when the soft and hard rocks, clay and other materials were first deposited into the area at the height of the flood, this 92,000 acre land mass was laid out as fairly level terrain, equal to the now existing height of the monuments themselves.

Since the area is so large and the monuments are some distance from one another, a view of the region from Muley Point in Utah, about 15 miles west of Mexican Hat, may help you to better understand what actually took place here. If you've never been there, just concentrate on what I am about to describe to you—hopefully you'll get the picture:

The receding floodwaters, as they were passing through this recent deposit with great force, washed, to a *considerable* depth, all of the loose sediments away, while the more rigid deposits held their ground. Tremendous masses of sediments as high as the current monuments were moved from this area as they were in all areas of the world during a five month period of water recession from the unimaginably high crest of the flood.

Though the more rigid deposits remained immovable, they were however shaped dramatically by the commanding persistence of retreating waters—the profound strokes of the Artist's brush. *All* of the monuments within this vast area have shale, pebble and sand deposits at their base. The bases themselves are gradually contoured outward.

When the high volume of receding waters significantly decreased, which according to the Biblical record took a minimum of five months, the bases of the newly formed monuments continued to remain under water for a period of time, which accounts for the watermarked contour visible on the base of each monument. The entire valley was a seemingly endless lake, while the newly formed monuments, at varying distances from one another, protruded up out of the shallow waters over several miles.

What an *overwhelmingly awesome sight* it must have been! A smaller version of this 'picture in time' exists still to this day, about 300 hundred miles to the west in the Lake Mead area, where separate red rock monuments protrude out of the waters there. Similar monuments are found in the water at various areas along the Colorado River, however, with the recession, the remaining floodwater in Monument Valley, which stands at a considerably higher elevation, was draining out—slowly *decreasing*. Over a period of time the earth eventually dried up in this higher area (Genesis 8:14), and Monument Valley was born.

It is indeed an inspiration to hike among the monuments of Monument Valley. When I do this I try to contemplate what actually took place here during its formation. The thought of it overturns the imagination. It is, of course, sacred ground. I couldn't look at it in any other way, nor can the local Indians.

Then again, all of the planet earth is sacred ground to the Christian, or at least it *should* be. But it is here, in this obviously immense moving and shaping of land, in this place where widespread, diversely yet harmoniously sculptured sentinels give glory to the One who formed them, where I fall on my face with exceedingly great thanksgiving in *awe* of the untold *wonder* of God, our Creator.

The first time Sandie and I went into the monuments we parked the trailer in a campsite that overlooked what the locals call, the *Mittens*. There are two formations. If you could see them you would understand why they were named as such. Across from them is another formation called *Merric Butte*. The three formations are pictured on postcards available from the Navajo Tribal Park, and are usually the scenery used for advertising the area in a variety of travel magazines.

While we stayed there, Sandie painted the exquisite desert scenery, which included all three of these formations, across the front awning (rock guard) of my trailer. The entire painting was about 6 feet wide and 2 feet in height. Her well-stroked work allowed me to take Monument Valley around with me, wherever I went. The Navajo's say that Monument Valley inspires us to 'walk in beauty.' I was allowed to '*live* in beauty' from that day on, thanks to Sandie's most fine reproduction of God's artwork.

Oh, the depth of the riches both of the wisdom and knowledge of God! How unsearchable are His judgments and His ways past finding out! (Romans 11:35 NKJV)

Into Death Valley

And they did not thirst when He led them through the deserts. He caused the waters to flow from the rock for them. He also split the rock, and the waters gushed out (Isaiah 48:21 NKJV).

Death Valley in California, perhaps at the bottom of a sea in the pre-flood world, is a notably vast formation of hills and buttes—an extremely picturesque mixture of multicolored sand, mud, clay and rocks. Water-carved arroyos and boulder strewn washes abound throughout this region, and hiking among them and through them is quite impressive, to say the least.

About 60 miles wide and over 125 miles in length, Death

Valley is still another true monument to God's creativity in the power of receding waters during the Great Flood of Noah. It is now however a very dry, still (quiet), and restful place. It is a medicinal location to set up camp under the stars or to leisurely dwell in during the day. I have been fortunate enough to have spent many rewardingly quiet times within its tranquil borders.

Quietness is indeed a good thing. The Bible teaches us; *in quietness and trust is your strength* (Isaiah 30:15 NKJV). Unfortunately, unending noise, most of it man made, pollutes life on our planet. Mankind rushes on not knowing their end, but when death comes there is truly nothing we can take with us save silence. The noise and futility of this life are left behind. Why not choose then to learn the value of living life here and now amidst quietness? Not externally of course, for that would be nearly impossible—unless you lived in a remote section of this desert.

I am talking here about *inner* quietness. Inner peace is developed through a learning process of trusting in God. It's something you just can't accomplish on your own. It is a reserved quietness, not tuned in to the world's noise. It is a result of knowing that God is in control—of accepting that life-giving fact within your heart and within your mind and within your spirit. He made all things, including you. There's great peace in that, for if He *formed* you, He will indeed *care* for you.

Lord, my heart is not proud. My eyes are not haughty. I do not concern myself with matters too great or awesome for me. But I have stilled and quieted myself, just as a small child is quiet with its mother. Yes, like a small child is my soul within me (Psalm 131 NKJV).

Inner peace, like all sound Biblical teachings regarding the principles of understanding, is developed through a timely learning process. It is the utopia in mind and body control. No man-made meditation practice can ever achieve it. You don't need to stand on your head in thought, nor contort your body through some man-inspired ritual, nor do you need to be an expert in Kung fu to obtain it. Inner peace comes only from a focus on God and a trust in God.

If you will, notice that the psalmist wrote that *he* had stilled and quieted *himself*. He had learned through experience not to be proud or self satisfied. His eyes were not haughty or arrogant or self-magnifying. He had become as a small child within his thinking, and he emphasized that. His focus and trust was in God (Psalm 131:3). Yes, he certainly had to find a resting place for the turmoil and cares of this life, both past and present, as well as find a refuge for the natural frustration of spirit encountered in achieving that particular quietness.

His trust then could have *only* been in God and not in himself, nor in human wisdom or philosophy. Only unwavering faith and trust *in God*, with patience, will develop that type of peace and quietness within. Contrary to the theories of modern psychology, there is, in pure reality, just no other way to go about it. The Bible teaches that the peace of God passes human understanding. We can obtain it if we are willing. Trust in God is the only attitude that can permanently conquer life's problems and difficulties. A God-centered attitude has power over all things.

You may have never been to Death Valley. There are many other similarly remote and quiet places all over the earth. Yet, if you have developed the quietness within which the psalmist speaks of, you could probably sit down in the median of a freeway during rush hour and be at peace. I wouldn't recommend that, but it is possible. Personally, I still prefer the external silence of the desert, the mountains, within a forest, or somewhere beside a quiet stream. These particular areas of God's creation 'speak' of His peace.

You might first take notice as to the silence of the rocks or the trees or the plants nearby as you wander about in these remote places. Believe me, if they could speak out in your language, they could teach you many things about God and inner quietness (Job 12:7-10). Death Valley is indeed one of those places where nature becomes your teacher. The quietness there is unique and may have something to do with the area's relation to sea level. It is the lowest point of land in the entire United States.

The Biblical book of Job teaches us in numerous passages that the *creation itself* trusts in God. That is why it is so quiet and peaceful within—following the natural order of life on the earth, remaining in subjection to its Creator. The creation itself knows that God is in control and will one day restore all things—including external peace (Romans 8:18-24). Learning more about the things that God has made, as well as the distinct peace He has endowed them with, can help you to trust in Him and to become at peace within yourself. You can become 'one with the earth' so to speak.

Again, you cannot rely on the teachings of men to still your soul, unless they are founded upon the Word of God. Allow me to share with you a 'tutoring' on inner peace from Death Valley, an area created for our inspiration by God during the Great Flood:

The terrain in Death Valley is indeed *rough*; much like the turmoil and frustration that goes with living in this world and much like who we are inside, yet the area itself we find to be still and peaceful. It has been quieted by time since the upheaval of the Great Flood, some 5000 years ago. An ancient waterbed, Death Valley is full of collectible rocks of all sizes, shapes and colors—indeed a rock hunter's paradise. Nowadays you're not supposed to remove them; just permitted to look at them.

There are hundreds of impressive water-laid canyons and arroyos here. Due to the natural environment of the area nearly 1000 species of plants flourish within its borders. To date there are at least twenty-one or more different species of plants that are found nowhere else in the world.[3] The valley is also home to many varieties of marsh grass. There are spectacular spring wildflower displays. There are numerous species of reptiles, birds and animals.

Once while journeying there, being occupied in a leisurely ascent of a multicolored rock butte, I was allowed the sudden honor of observing a most handsome and interesting desert specimen—a coyote. As I rounded an outcropping of rock, I spotted him on the narrow ridge just ahead of me. The rarely hiked and washed out trail that I was on bore a weathered posting at its trailhead—'Hike or Die.' I had made the right choice—I kept on moving forward in the desert heat.

He saw me immediately and stopped in his track to investigate my intrusion into his domain. I felt 'at one' with him for a moment—we were both alone in a remote area of exceptional inspiration. He took a few steps away from me, then stopped and turned his head back to observe me once again. He then gracefully moved his body around, facing me head-on. He was indeed very healthy looking for a desert coyote. His hair was coarse and colorful and his size well above average. He stood so majestically there, an air of gentle boldness about him. I was of course quite thrilled by his presence—actually, beyond measure.

I instinctively said, "Hello," to him. He perked up his ears and continued to watch me. I wasn't sure that he'd ever had the English language spoken at him before. I then climbed on around toward the ridge approaching him, just below his perch, and continued on my journey, stepping down on a somewhat lower outcrop of red rock and passing by just underneath him. I could have reached up and nearly touched him. He kept watch on me for a short period as I did on him, then he turned and moved on, crossing a sloped expanse of red rock, bound in another direction from me.

He came to a dead stop once on that journey and looked back, as if to say, "Farewell—watch yourself out here, man—snakes about." He continued on after that and I soon lost sight of him among the rocks. I called out to him, but he did not come into my view again. He had appeared the whole time that I was allowed the honor of His presence to be very untroubled, not at all apprehensive like most coyotes I have come in contact with in the wilderness. Perhaps it is Death Valley itself that inspired the behavior of this particular coyote.

The valley is indeed quite captivating in nature, breathtakingly still, full of some of God's finest artwork; beyond any shadow of doubt a most adequate tutor on spiritual nourishment. You can actually take a deep breath and smell the strength of the *enriching quietness* in this place. Realms of quietness have distinct scents of their own—did you know that? The Apache Indians teach us that stillness is an *unequaled* pleasure. This is of course all God's doing.

You can develop the very same quietness and stillness within yourself; an inner peace that passes understanding (Philippians 4:6,7). It is a process of training your attitudes and your senses in learning to rightly appreciate God's wonders—a process of giving 'thanks' as you learn to trust Him in and for your daily walk, carrying those wonders along with you in your heart and mind. The psalmist well understood this concept.

Within Death Valley there is a road named *Artist Drive*, where oxidation has produced a rainbow of colors in the eroded clay deposits of ancient ocean or lake bed sediments. The colors are most intense during late afternoon. *Artists Palette*, about halfway along the drive, is a particularly unusual mosaic of red, yellow, orange, green, violet, brown and black hues. Being an artist, Sandie was most inspired in this area. To me, it looks like the place where God may have mixed his paints for the entire valley. Whether it is or not, it is encouraging to think of it in that way.

The Lord is my shepherd; I shall not be in want. He makes me to lie down in green pastures; He leads me beside quiet waters. He restores my soul... (Psalm 23:1-3 NKJV).

Listening to the Wind

Who can this be, that even the wind and the sea obey Him? (Mark 4:41 NKJV)

Hello, from the vast and beautiful Arizona desert. I've been allowed to travel around the West for several years now, working at various campgrounds, doing some writing, teaching and hiking amidst breathtaking, God-sculptured scenery, while at the same time experiencing many extremely valuable lessons that God has so graciously taught me along the way. However, there

have been some times when I wasn't quite sure where I was going spiritually.

You know how we are sometimes not sure about things in our mind, traveling that road of human uncertainty? I was once told by an American Indian (Sioux) that when I am walking with uncertainty, I need to stop and "listen to the wind." There was a time when I would have thought that he meant that I should just blow on out and away from wherever I was and whatever I was

thinking and forget about uncertainty.

But we do fear change, unfamiliar circumstances, new

beginnings, don't we? And, most of us are not use to listening to the trees or talking to the sand to get answers. There are indeed many who think that this particular type of advice is strange—to listen to the wind. Yet, true Christians are supposed to be born of the Spirit (John 3:5). Jesus himself describes one born of the Spirit in John 3, verse 8:

Just as you can hear the wind but can't tell where it comes from or where it is going, so it is with those who are born of the Spirit (NKJV).

It is true; we cannot physically pinpoint the Spirit of God. We cannot tell where it comes from, nor can we determine where it goes. But, we can hear it. Like the wind, His spirit moves over the deserts and plains, over the fields, the mountains and the waters. We can see its affect in nature and on the environment. It can also speak to us within our hearts, within our inner man (or woman), in unsearchable ways (1st Corinthians 2:10-16). If we are listening with our hearts and become obedient to His Spirit, we can see its affect on our lives as well.

This particular Arizona desert region that we are hiking along the Colorado River is surrounded by lofty, pointed buttes. It is full of numerous canyons and colorful hills. There are sandy, rock-strewn washes containing many varieties of desert brush. It is obviously an area blessed with a medley of winds. Winds carry the seeds from existing plants to produce even more plants, allowing the desert to become a lush wilderness. These winds can be soft and gentle, gusty and strong, relentless in nature, and are always unpredictable with their sudden changes in direction. They also speak.

They speak of the ancient Flood and of its diverse marks on the land. They encircle the mountains among these craggy peaks, boastfully threatening them with their demonstration of immeasurable, usurping power. They reshape the hills, seed the ground and carve the dunes. They whisper the dramatic stories of ancient patriarchs who dwelt in similar topography. They tell of warriors and shepherds, of kings and queens, of princes and nomads, of explorers and pioneers, and serve to encourage the weary, lonely desert wanderer.

The winds forever speak of God's presence. They build the foundations for the clouds, moving them into gorgeous sunrises and sunsets. Yes, this desert is indeed a remarkably inspiriting area for *listening to the wind*. If you are like me and love the caress of God against your face, then this is the place to be. God can reach out and touch you in a marvelous way through His elements of snow, wind and rain. What encouragement and inspiration His wonders can bestow upon you!

Winds do not speak of cities, of high-rise buildings nor other man-made structures. They don't talk of dams or power plants. They don't whisper of trains or of airplanes or of automobiles, or of modern technology in any form. Their conversation is not of this world. Being spiritual in nature, winds could care less about those particularly earthly things. They do, as I mentioned before, speak to the waters and could overthrow the land and destroy its structures and its inhabitants, at any time, in any number of ways.

Yet, winds are prone to God's mercy and do not overrule His established boundaries (Psalm135:7). They were created by Him and therefore operate by His authority (Psalm 147:18). The winds have understanding as well as might; they are *lovingly obedient* in all ways to the Lord their creator. They know their place in God's natural order of things and speak in accordance with His will. They do His will, but beware; they are permitted, with limitations imposed by God, to also do the will of Satan (Job 1:19).

And so, being as diverse and influential as they are, they can be truly uplifting in spirit and uniquely instructive to one whose desire is to listen to them. As the wind can be a reminder to us of God's presence, it is also a reminder for us that God is in control. My daughter recently spoke to me of her experience in viewing the results of a tornado in a rural Ohio town. Profoundly, she was more concerned about identifying the purpose of God's work, if it was indeed God's work, than in contemplating the value of material losses among her relatives and neighbors.

Incidentally, that tornado struck with great devastation on all sides of her home, but did not so much as lift a shingle on her house. Even if it would have struck her house, I am confident, through an understanding of her mindset regarding this event, that she is one who listens to and has understanding regarding the wind. Her obvious respect and growing love toward her Creator and His sovereignty have allowed her great insight—she is aware of who is in control and confident in His judgments.

Listening to the wind is not really strange advice after all:

Who but God goes up to heaven and comes back down? Who holds the wind in His fists? Who wraps up the oceans in His cloak? Who has created the whole wide world? What is His name—and His Son's name? Tell me if you know! (Proverbs 30:4 NLT)

Desert Prayer

Charge Joshua and encourage him and strengthen him, for he shall go across at the head of his people (Deuteronomy 3:28 NASB).

We're camping in the great eastern Mojave Desert region of southern California. It's morning and last night's campfire is just simmering coals now, but adequate for brewing trail coffee. It is easy here in this wilderness, with that cup of trail coffee in hand, to hike a short distance from the trailer and find myself within the shield of a deep ravine, with no man made objects in sight.

One might think that it would be mighty lonely out here, and

I do sincerely miss various friends and family, yet, I am *encouraged* nonetheless. What I have is the *encouragement* of rugged desert topography, all around me, and the vast, open sky above me. It is indeed beautiful here and extremely quiet as well.

Though it should be first and foremost, encouragement is not something you always find among people out there in the world. It is indeed like pure gold—a hard find. But with God, encouragement is available on a daily basis—even out here in the desert. When and if you seek encouragement, honoring its heavenly source, you will surely find it.

A variety of brush grows here in the desert, which is now in gorgeous bloom. Sand washes and multicolored rocks abound. Rolling hills and pointed buttes are indeed impressive as well. Most importantly, I am alone with God amidst these wonders—a fine place to be in the morning. His creation is the very first thing I face, and the awesomeness, as well as the stillness, is an extreme pleasure. My thoughts are drawn toward Him immediately; I give thanks for the air that I breathe and the desert scents that I smell.

I thank Him for my sight; that He has allowed me to behold yet another glorious morning among His wonders. I look down at my hiking boots on the desert terrain and give thanks that I have been allowed to walk on His sacred earth. The worries of the day have not crept in as of yet, and the warmth of His mercy, which is new every morning (Lamentations 3:23), now surrounds me. I am therefore encouraged beyond understanding (Philippians 4:7).

I descend to my knees and ask for His strength so that I might endure this day among the human inhabitants of the earth, with the majority of their minds so far from Him. I ask that I might be allowed to continue to think of Him, so that I myself can survive the day. I have learned to understand that the world was formed by Him, that I was formed by Him, and so as I walk out of this protective ravine I am encouraged that, no matter what I am about to face this day, I can endure because He is with me; guarding me, guiding me, all the day, all the way; something I didn't realize at all in my youth.

I cannot turn back the hands of time, but I am indeed thankful for this present knowledge of Him. He does not hold yesterday against me. If I am willing, He will walk with me each day of my life. The gift of this knowledge and the faith it can generate is the *absolute elite* in encouragement. Among what friends or relations will you find this extreme height of encouragement?

On the earth it is impossible, yet, with God, all things are possible (Mark 10:27). You can draw from this higher level by allowing the Spirit of God to work through you, and you can give the gift of such encouragement to friends or relations—to anyone with whom you come in contact. No matter where you live, no matter where or what you have been, no matter who you are, no matter what your circumstance and no matter how deep your scars or how repulsive the stains of your sins, you *can be* an encourager. You can create encouragement.

You were designed to create! You can also encourage and inspire the creative abilities within others. Those who criticize can create nothing. There are those who believe in 'constructive criticism'. To the contrary, *all* criticism is *destructive*. We therefore need to turn our negative criticism into positive encouragement. We have each been given the *opportunity* to create. We were each created in God's image, thereby giving us the *ability* to create. As our talents vary, so our creativity varies. We, each and every one of us, have something unique to offer— something 'different' to add to encouragement.

The earthly Webster defined encouragement as follows: To inspire with courage, hope or resolution. To help or to foster (promote) growth or development. In other words it means to *build up*. As God encourages us (*builds us up*), we need also to encourage (*build up*) others. We need to ask His help when speaking to others. We need to ask Him to guard our thoughts and our intentions.

We need carefully then to *season* our words and/or actions toward others. We need the right 'flavor' in speaking or acting. The Bible describes the 'right words spoken' as *spiritual weapons* with the ability to *knock down* the devil's strongholds, to *capture rebels and bring them back to God* (2nd Corinthians 10:2-5, italicized for emphasis).

Properly seasoned, words can be indeed powerful! It is vitally important then to take the time to commune with God before or even while you're interacting and/or conversing with others. Also, when you are alone at night, go over the day's events with Him. Confess your faults and ask Him to help you in applying His counsel toward others and to guard your tongue in this process.

No one of course can tame the tongue (James 3:8), but, by increasing this practice of communing with God, it is through Him that you can gain the wisdom and understanding needed to *control* your tongue. You can indeed be developed into a productive tool of creative encouragement.

You can also help through sharing your life, your worldly goods, your active talents and seasoned speech; to inspire and to motivate the creativity in others. This sharing of your life, of your goods and of your talents, is an element of *love*, something we all need so desperately to do. Keep in mind that everything you have has been given you from above (John 19:11). You are the steward of each of the things you have been given.

There are a lot of folk's out there who have no homes, no daily bread, and many who have never even heard a kind word spoken. This should not be. These folk's don't need the world nor what it offers—they need you. Try then not to lose patience in your continued endeavors to make the world a better place for those along your path.

Go often to your favorite retreat, or to any place where you can engage in quiet prayer and seek the Lord's help. His encouragement toward you, *freely given to you*, is your greatest power for the influence of goodness toward others. Encouragement can make all the difference in the world in one's life. Pray that He will strengthen you in your efforts to *encourage* others…

And after He had sent the multitudes away, He went up to the mountain by himself to pray (Matthew 14:23 NASB).

Looks like our early morning campfire is close to burning out. Perhaps we had just better let it be and build a new one tonight. Coffee's lukewarm, but you're welcome to a little. We'll be headin' out shortly to view some of the desert's finest creatures. That's coming up in chapter 4.

Thanks so much for hiking with me along the *Desert Trail*. I trust your trek was well worthwhile. Come back anytime and we'll do it again. Bring some friends along. Anyone is welcome here…

My pal, Digger

Chapter Four...**Ask the Animals**

Ask the animals and they will teach you, or the birds of the air, and they will tell you; or speak to the earth, and it will teach you, or let the fish of the sea inform you. Which of all these does not know that the hand of the Lord has done this? In His hand is the life of every creature and the breath of all mankind (Job 12:7-10 NIV).

There's a *little* dog (pictured above) that happens to be a *big* part of my life. He's a Chihuahua, the cutest little guy you've ever seen. His name is *Digger*, and he has taught me more about the *character* of God's love than any other creature on the face of the earth. I am indeed indebted to him.

He has taught me of faithfulness and loyalty, of kindness and gentleness, of patience and forgiveness, and most importantly, he has taught me the deep meaning of friendship and love, which is actually a combination of all of the above. The question is, who taught him these things? No mistake about it—the opening Scripture for this chapter definitely answers that question.

Digger's character had a designer. In order for Digger to be who he is, it only stands to reason that his designer would himself have to possess an abundance of these very qualities. And, the designer would award Digger with these qualities, that I might better comprehend, in accordance with the Scripture, the attributes of the designer—through Digger.

This animal would serve to teach me something very special about the Lord, who made all things. How much more then should I embrace the desire to teach my fellow man/woman these things? Get the picture? By the way, *altruism* (unselfish concern for others) contradicts evolution. I might add that *spontaneous generation* (the emergence of life from nonliving matter) has *never* been observed.

Life comes only from life, not through natural processes as evolution claims. Forget that theory—it is a product of the imaginations of ignorant men and one of Satan's greatest tools used to cloud your mind. Don't be deceived—Digger's existence and character prove the theory of organic evolution to be absolutely false. He is just about the most unselfish character I have ever known, indeed a reflection of his Creator.

Digger is *faithful*. By his own free will he comes to me at all times, no matter what I am doing, no matter what my mood, and lays at my feet in a position of both submissiveness and contentment. He seems to relish being around me at all times, especially when lying upon my lap. You can always count on him to be an encourager.

He is *loyal*. If I get up and move somewhere, he follows, no matter where I may go—upstairs, downstairs, you name it, he's on my heals at all times. If I am coming in from outside, he always waits with excitement at the door when he hears me approach. If a stranger approaches, he is quick to warn me with a loud bark.

He is *kind*. He licks my fingers in affection when I reach down to touch him, or licks my face when I hold him in my arms. He warms up to strangers when he senses that they are not a threat. He shares his water with other dogs, wagging his tail as he watches them lap it from his dish. He smiles—and you can see it.

He is *gentle*. When he jumps upon my bed and climbs onto my chest, he relaxes, then raises one leg (his right arm) in an act of submissiveness. He submits completely whenever I stoke his back or simply touch him anywhere. When playfully chewing on my fingers with his sharp teeth, he never resorts to a pressure that would injure my flesh.

He is *patient*. He watches me when I eat, sometimes motionless and without wavering, waiting for some morsel that I might grant him. When his need is to go outside, he sits at the door and patiently waits for me to respond. He relaxes in complete comfort while being bathed or having his claws trimmed.

He is *forgiving*. If I should speak harshly at him, which I no longer even consider, he immediately cowers and lowers his head for a moment, but then approaches me and wags his tail, ready to display his love once again. If I accidentally step on his foot (he is small and you don't always realize he is there), he will give a yelp, but immediately draws near to me again, as if to say, "That's okay, I'm okay."

Naturally Digger is a little mischievous and even ornery at times—he's a victim of the Fall, as all animals are. Yet, God has allowed His unfathomable love to work through Digger on my behalf, restraining him from many of his natural traits. Let me take that concept just a little deeper:

God knows all things from beginning to end. Every moment of our individual lives are in His hands and have been from our very conception within the mother's womb that he chose for us. Our lives are then of course lived out within the framework of our parent's choices and eventually our own choices. These choices sometime wrestle against God's purpose and result in us wandering in the wilderness for a time, but God is not at all thwarted in bringing about His purpose for us.

Though we are rebellious, He continues His work for us—and works relentlessly. He uses any means available in accomplishing His will, *always* having His best interest for us at heart. For me, I believe *one* of those 'means' happens to be a member of His animal kingdom, which concept is certainly upheld in the opening Scripture of this chapter; *ask the animals and they shall teach you…*

Digger has taught me how important it is to spend time with him, and he respects and values every moment of that time. He has caused me to consider my failures in this realm with my human children many years ago. By that I mean that he has taught me the importance of each *moment* in life. He has taught me how much I have missed by not making use of significant moments in that former relationship. Had I been like Digger in character in my youth, my family would still be intact. The children would of course be grown up and long gone by now, pursuing their own destinies, but my life with them could have been much different—precious moments spent with them would have made a world of difference—in their lives as well as mine.

They could have known an unmatched closeness with both their mother and their father. I could have taught them what love is, as Digger has taught me. I would have known how to truly *listen* to each word that came out of the mouth of every member of my family. I would have known how to reply to them with tenderness and understanding. I would have been the rock that they could have depended upon, no matter what life dealt. I would have been the shepherd that they could have looked up to for encouragement, for hope, and for protection. And, unless I died, they would have *known* that 'daddy' was never going anywhere—that I was their counselor and friend for life.

Digger is a creature that lives moment by moment. Everything seems important to him; touching him, talking to him, playing with him, walking with him and allowing him to run through the grass and among the flowers of the field, sniffing everything in sight in total awareness of his surroundings—for each of these things he is extremely grateful. He knows how to make the most of every moment. To top it all off, he trusts in me moment to moment—he knows that God gave me authority over him. That particular trust is indeed humbling, allowing me insight into the deeper intrinsic values of responsibility.

He doesn't even consider running away from me under any circumstance. If a big ol' dog growls at him, he just stands erect like Rin Tin Tin and faces the oppressor head on—size matters not. If the oppressor moves toward him, he is quick to retreat and stand between my legs. He knows that I'm the guy who will protect him. His trust makes me aware of the great responsibility we as humans have toward the animal kingdom, yet, how much more then should we consider our relationship to others of the human race?

Moments are significant in any relationship. A moment by moment awareness of *words* we are about to speak, of *affections* we choose to bestow, of *behavior* we are about to display, and the *encouragement* that we need to give are the most important considerations in human relationships that we can *ever* contemplate.

Dear reader, life *does* need to be lived moment by moment—with faithfulness, loyalty, kindness, gentleness, patience and forgiveness. These are the qualities that can make your family members your best friends. These qualities serve also to make you a best friend to others. These qualities display integrity, yet are but a mere shadow of God's qualities, which indeed serve to make Him the very best of your friends. He is a friend who sticks closer than a brother (Proverbs 18:24). He is the One upon whose lap we are permitted to rest—where our trust in Him becomes our greatest security.

Behold all of the wonders this *friend* has created for you! Behold the sky, the sun, the moon, the stars, the mountains, the deserts, the canyons, the plants and flowers! Can His character— His attributes become any clearer to you? Only the insensitively ignorant would not want to imitate Him. We would be wise to desire the mind of Christ—to imitate Him through our words and actions (Philippians 2:5, Matthew 11:29) on a daily, moment by moment basis. We can learn to love in spite of our proneness to sin, for love covers (*holds at bay*) a multitude of sins (1st Peter 4:8).

Consider all that God has put into the heart of little Digger, who is just a grain of sand among all the animals! You can see that, when the Spirit of God moves in the heart, goodness is indeed produced. God teaches us what love is using a myriad of sources available to Him; and through Him, if we do not quench His Spirit within us, we can radiate this love that He so graciously bestows upon us.

The animals know, the birds know, the fish of the sea know, even the *stones* cry out! (Luke 19:40) The earth is also aware—it can teach you that the hand of the Lord has made all of these things—including you! And you are the *crown* of His creation— you are the love of His life (Psalm 8:5). Why not learn to love Him in return?

There have been times at particular moments during the writing of this book that I have encountered depression. When I consider the world that I live in and the earthly attitudes that are prevalent in society, I wonder if my efforts are actually worth the effort? Is this writing from a sinner, whose eyes have been opened, really going to make a difference—is it going to help someone else? Will the attributes of our Creator become more visible to one who reads this book? Will certain truths catch hold of a reader and allow him/her to gain the understanding needed to motivate them for the betterment of themselves and others?

The last time these thoughts overwhelmed me I sat at my desk in silence for some time. I had been working on this very chapter. I also took notice that Digger was at my feet the whole time, lying in a position of contentment, his big, beautiful eyes fixed gently upon me.

When I reached down to acknowledge him, I realized that his presence was an encouragement—what he taught me about his Creator was expected to be shared with the human race—my entire life's experience of learning in all areas of living was to be bestowed upon others for a reason. Digger's humble presence reminded me that I needed to 'stay the course' in my endeavor and not lose heart. I realized also that this animal had truly become a part of my personal connection with God...

We're still out here in the middle of the desert right now—still listening to the wind. There are no schedules, no meetings, no pressures out here—just raw time. Time to watch. Time to listen in depth. Time to think about God, and time to talk with the animals—and ask them. After all, they were made from the earth as well (Genesis 1:24).

Let us consider what the Biblical book of Job has offered us for our instruction and encouragement. Let us hike around out here and observe just a few of the desert's more popular inhabitants[2] and learn something from each of them, shall we? Perhaps you are one of those folk's who may connect with God in this way...

Coyotes

The first desert creature I want you to observe today is the Coyote. Lots of 'em out here in the desert. One of the most adaptable animals in the world, the Coyote can change its breeding habits, diet and social dynamics to survive a wide variety of habitats. It is an opportunistic, persistent and extremely elusive predator, skilled in a variety of hunting techniques. It travels over its range and hunts both day and night, running swiftly and catching its prey easily. The Coyote is extremely intelligent in that it honors all attributes given it by the Creator.

Here in the desert its principle diet is composed of mice, rabbits, ground squirrels and other small rodents, insects, reptiles, and fruits and berries of wild plants. While hunting for food the Coyote's hearing is very acute and is used for detecting prey and avoiding danger. With an excellent sense of smell the Coyote tracks its prey, then usually stalks it for 20-30 minutes before pouncing. A Coyote can run at nearly 40 miles per hour. It has the stamina to chase its prey over long distances and then can strike when the quarry is exhausted. They are however truly much more than just great hunters.

Of all the wild animals on our planet they are an outstanding example of devotion to family. They are ideal parents, sharing with their spouse the responsibility of feeding and raising their young ones. In their dens they are loving, loyal, and most willing to work together for the common good. I'm not a family man at this time, but if I were I would take lessons from the mature domestic qualities of the Coyote.

How I wish I would have wandered the deserts in my earlier years and learned both the value and application of these meaningful qualities! I'm sure it would have produced in me the wisdom to be a much better communicator, provider, and leader to and for the family God gave me.

Coyotes use a variety of calls to defend their territory, as well as for strengthening social bonds and general communication. I have heard them 'calling' in great numbers. If you go into their territory and call out in a similar fashion, the

Coyotes will indeed call out to you in return. I experienced this most unique communication many times while working high in the Angeles Forest with Hal Deckhert, one of my campground work associates. We were fortunate to get our 'talking to the coyotes' experiences on videotape.

A lot of folk's think of Coyotes only as savages and scavengers. When these folk's hear the call of the Coyote, the hair usually stands up on the back of their necks. But, to the seasoned outdoorsman or the Native American, the howl of the Coyote is truly a song of the West. The animal's finer qualities go virtually untold, one of them being that Coyotes are quite necessary in preserving the balance of nature. We are indeed fortunate that the night song of the 'Little Wolf' may still be heard throughout the desert southwest. There is much one can glean from the observation and study of these incredible animals.

Jack Rabbits

The black-tailed Jack Rabbit, a desert dweller, is found in all four southwestern American deserts. Its diet is strictly vegetation, such as shrubs, creosote bushes, mesquite trees, snake weeds, junipers, big sagebrush's and cacti. The Jack Rabbit eats constantly and doesn't require much water, as it obtains nearly all the water it needs from the plant material it eats—they're great harvesters, and preserve the balance of nature in the desert by spreading seed.

Jack Rabbits are born bright eyed, active soon after birth and ready to fend for themselves in just 30 days. They reach adult size in seven to eight months. They are more active in the evening as their eyes focus well at night. They are always aware of their surroundings, and in addition to this keen eyesight, rely on acute hearing and swift zigzag running to insure their safety and survival. They can leap as far as fifteen feet, reaching speeds up to 50 miles per hour in their escape. They are nearly twice as elusive as the cottontail rabbit.

Also unlike the cottontail rabbit they are not found in the more easy to menace social groups. Jack Rabbits are solitary creatures. This tends to make them quite good at survival. Unfortunately they are sometimes the victim of predators, such as bobcats, foxes, horned owls, eagles, hawks, snakes and coyotes. The victimization of this gentle creature reminds me of John the baptist, who was a cousin of Jesus of Nazareth.

John spent his life in the desert. He was a solitary individual whose diet was locusts and wild honey. He went about dressed in camel hair clothing—a lowly man honorably called to prepare the way for the coming of Jesus and the kingdom of God. Many of the common people loved him, but he was indeed hated by the religious leaders of his day. He was eventually caged in prison at a young age and beheaded through the vindictiveness of an evil predator, the wife of a king.

Though John would have been despised in today's world—dressed in camel hair and living like a transient in the remoteness of the desert—Jesus declared him to be the greatest man ever born (Matthew 11:8-11). He was indeed a wise harvester, winning many souls back to God, yet he was a man of simple means. To have any of his qualities today, including his love for the wilderness and his ability to adapt to it, would be indeed a great honor.

Locusts

Locusts, who frequent the desert, are mentioned far more times than all the other insects of the Bible *combined*. There's much to learn from these small but enlightened creatures. Allow me to give you just a few insights into their characteristics. The average swarm of Locusts is made up of 40 billion individuals, who eat 40 million pounds of food a day.

The largest recorded swarm to date was two thousand miles long, and had an estimated population of 250 billion Locusts. That particular swarm could have eaten 250 million pounds of food a day. They are considered mostly to be destroyers. They are unbelievably devastating when in such unity. Their food is vegetation, most of which is for human consumption.

Surprisingly, Locusts do not have any leaders—no king—yet they march like an army in ranks (Proverbs 30:27). The Proverbs also teach us that Locusts are one of four things on earth that are small, but unusually wise (Proverbs 30:24). When Locusts swarm they go in the same direction and do the same thing, accomplishing a common goal without any leadership. Unity in the *right* direction is indeed wise. Much can be accomplished by working together.

God gives us this proverbial picture of unity through the activity of the Locusts. We don't need a human king to accomplish what we were created for (1ˢᵗ Samuel 8:6,7). If we would all have as our purpose to love and to serve God rather than ourselves, we could accomplish many things that we are at present unable to accomplish (John 15:5). God also makes a wonderful promise to us using Locusts in a spiritual application:

I will restore to you the years that the swarming locusts have eaten, the crawling locust, the consuming locust, and the chewing locust (Joel 2:25 NKJV). God is ready to forgive you of your many failures and to restore (bring healing to) the years lost in the hardships that life has dealt, if you are but willing.

Owls

Great Horned Owls, whose feather tufts above the ears appear as 'horns', often spend their winters protected by the rocks and crags of desert canyons. The Owls are birds of prey, hunting rodents and other small animals. These great birds can reach as much as 22 inches in length. Their "hoot" is a classic sound of the wild, and like the coyote, can be heard a long way off. It is still another 'song of the West'.

They are also great parents, both male and female fiercely defending their nest site against intruders. If young Owls fall out of their nest prematurely, the adults will both feed and protect the birds on the ground. When Owls awaken, they use their hearing and eyesight to alert them of danger or possible prey.

Great horned Owl's eyes, which are almost as large as humans, allow an abundant amount of light to pass through the pupil so that the Owl can see well in dark conditions. If one of these Owls were as big as a human in bodily stature, each of its eyes would be the size of a small grapefruit! However, their eyes are fixed in the sockets and cannot be moved up or down nor from side to side. They are able to rotate their head 270 degrees to compensate for this fixed condition of their eyes.

They also have an incredible sense of hearing. They use triangulation to pinpoint the source of a sound when their prey cannot be seen. By tilting or moving their head until the sound is of equal volume in each ear, the Owl can pinpoint the direction and distance of the sound quite accurately. The Owl's facial disk is shaped like a shallow bowl. This shape acts like a satellite dish, to help funnel sound into the ear openings.

The Owl is indeed unique in its appearance. Throughout history and across many cultures people have regarded Owls with fascination and awe. Among the different American Indian tribes there are various beliefs regarding the Owl. According to Navajo legend, the Creator told the Owl that men would listen to its voice to learn what would be their future. To the Apache warriors, dreaming of an Owl signified approaching death. The Ogallala Sioux allowed warriors who had excelled in battle to wear a cap of Owl feathers to signify their bravery.

The Sioux also believed that the forces of nature would favor those who wore Owl feathers, and that their vision (both physical and spiritual) would be increased. But the Sioux medicine men warned that to actually see an Owl meant that someone, other than the observer, was about to die. The Cheyenne of the Great Plains believe that the Owl represents the north wind.

In England, it's supposedly good luck to see an Owl. That Owls are like gods, with knowledge and wisdom, is a legend of Greek origin. The Romans wrote that the Owl could only foretell evil and are to be dreaded more than all other birds. Each of these legends, as well as hundreds of others, portrays the Owl as a creature that apparently possesses special powers not found in other animals.

It is truly one of the most honored of birds. Being a creation of God, the Owl is of course even wiser than we have come to think. Legends aside, there is much we can learn from a study of the Owl regarding its unique features, habits and abilities.

Sheep

Sheep receive more attention in the Bible than any other animal. They were important in the domestic, civic, and religious life of the Israelites. The earliest mention of Sheep is in Genesis 4:2, where it is said that "Abel was a keeper of Sheep." This was quite early in the creation, as Abel was one of Adam's children, who continued to honor God's love through caring for His creatures.

The shepherd's integral care is beautifully portrayed in the 23rd Psalm. This continuous care of the Sheep eventually led the early shepherds to know each one in their flock by name. Sheep were always led and never driven; they relied completely upon their shepherd for guidance.

Occasionally shepherdesses cared for Sheep as in the case of the seven daughters of the priest of Midian, whom Moses assisted at a well. Water wells were important meeting places for tribesmen (and women) and their flocks in those days. Both good and poor (or 'bad') shepherds are mentioned in the Bible, and during the latter parts of Israel's history their leaders were moreover denounced as being *bad* shepherds.

Figures of speech concerning Sheep and shepherding were used repeatedly as God warned His people of their shortcomings. Through this guidance God became known as the *Shepherd of His people*. Jesus Christ came to earth as the Good Shepherd and His arrival was announced, not in broad daylight to the government of Rome or to the Jewish religious leaders, but to humble shepherds who were watching their flocks by night in the fields. God sees not as man sees nor pays attention to the ranking order of men, but in righteousness (*doing things right*) respects the humble and lowly.

Sheep were kept for their milk more than for their flesh. Yet the common breed could store a vast amount of fat in the tail and this was used as food. They also provided wool for clothing and blankets, and horns; used either for carrying oil or wine, or as trumpets for summoning the people together. Horns were also used in religious rites. The skins of rams were used in making the covering of the tabernacle. Of course, Sheep were also used in sacrifice. Offerings consisted not only of lambs but also of ewes and rams.

The ultimate sacrifice was the Lamb of God, who in many respects was foreshadowed by the ways in which lambs had served as sacrifices throughout the centuries before Christ. Jesus was the Lamb of God, who took away the sins of the world, sacrificed according to God's plan that would allow us to be saved through Him. He was led like a Sheep to the slaughter, and as a lamb before the shearer is silent, so He did not open His mouth (Acts 8:32).

There was a time in my life when I didn't pay much attention to Sheep. Now, I am deeply inspired by them. God in His kindness has given me that inspiration. Each time I observe a flock in the desert or its adjacent fields, I search out the young lambs and watch them at play. I want to pick them up and cuddle them in my arms. I thank God for giving me this warm desire to care for each of His creatures. I always consider and long to imitate the gentleness of the Lamb—the One who cared enough to give His life for me.

Ravens

There are many Ravens out here in the desert. These scavengers go most everywhere and will eat just about anything; dead and decaying meat, rodents, insects and rotten garbage left by inconsiderate hikers and campers. They are what we would consider 'nasty birds,' as they store their food in animal dung, in order to prevent it from freezing during the winter. They also sift through various kinds of animal dung in search of tasteful dung beetles. We humans have for centuries considered them a disgusting bird, associating them with filth, evil and horror.

It is interesting to note however that Ravens are considered to be the most *intelligent* of all birds. A Raven will drop a walnut in front of an oncoming car, allowing it to be crushed in order to devour its meat. They are indeed problem solvers. God honored the Ravens when He allowed them to bring food to His servant, Elijah, who was hiding in a barren desert from the wrath of a vicious King Ahab (1st Kings 17:6).

The Ravens brought Elijah bread and meat in the morning and bread and meat in the evening. We are not told how long Elijah stayed in the desert, but he didn't leave until a brook he was drinking from there had dried up. The Ravens fed him until the very day he left. When I see the Ravens I think of this enduring story, of the so-called 'disgusting birds' that kept one of God's greatest servants alive.

It also serves to remind me of how much God has cared for me over the years. Two Ravens visited me on a daily basis recently when I was camping alone in a desolate area. They were indeed a great comfort, and I was allowed the honor of feeding them each day. The Scriptures teach us to consider the Ravens; they do not plant or harvest, they don't have storehouses or barns to put food in, yet our heavenly Father feeds them. This teaching concludes by saying that we humans are of far more value to Him than many birds (Luke 12:24).

Though these creatures appear to have some strange habits, they are due our respect and admiration, as are all of God's creatures. There is a dire warning in the Scriptures concerning Ravens: *The eye that mocks his father, and scorns obedience to his mother, the ravens of the valley will pluck it out* (Proverbs 30:17 NKJV).

As a boy my mother use to tell me that if I were disobedient, the birds would pluck out my eyes. Now I know where she got that idea—it did keep me on my toes, and I am thankful to this day for that wise admonition.

Snakes

One of the first things I ever saw out here in the desert was a Snake. A big ol' buck rattler. I remember at that very moment recalling what Jesus had said, 'be as wise as the serpent' (Matthew 10:16). When God made the creatures of the earth He made the Snake more subtle than any of the other creatures (Genesis 3:1).

During the whole of its life the Snake never closes its eyes. It cannot because God designed it without eyelids. A Snake keeps watch 24 hours a day, every day, 365 days of the year. The Snake sleeps, but its eyes continue to see objects that might affect its safety and survival. For example, if a Snake were napping on a rock and a leaf fell from a nearby tree within the Snake's field of vision, the Snake would remain asleep.

But, if the Snake were to see the shape of a hawk, a coyote, an eagle or some other predator, it would awaken and crawl to safety. That's the ultimate in observation. It is something we humans need to learn to do with regard to the cunning deceitfulness of Satan, that serpent of old, who can be lying around while we're unaware, in a watchful endeavor to destroy us (Psalm 37:32). But snakes are not only observant; they're also very sensitive—feeling oriented.

The viper has a labial pit on each side of its face, inside of which is a heat-sensitive nerve. There are many times when a viper crawls through high grass and cannot see its prey. Yet, the Snake can *feel* better than it can see. The viper turns its head from side to side until each heat-sensitive nerve detects the same temperature. It can sense a quarter-degree of temperature difference five feet away. If it strikes at a heat source while its nerves are experiencing the same temperature, it will hit the source with deadly accuracy. Missile guidance systems were designed after the heat-sensing capability of the viper. These systems were first used to guide the so-called *Sidewinder* missiles.

The Snake has a unique way of finding food. As it crawls it licks the air with its narrow, forked tongue. The tongue has a sticky substance that attracts molecules in the air. When the Snake withdraws its tongue and rubs it across a sensing organ within its mouth, it is able to classify particular molecules. If adequate quantities exist, the Snake knows he's got something. He then curls up and waits for the chance to snatch his prey. Snakes have remarkable patience and endurance. They can remain motionless without eating or drinking for months.

Snakes are at their best after they have been exposed to light for a time. They are cold blooded by nature, but can and do adapt to the surrounding temperatures. The colder they are the slower they move and the less likely they are to catch food. If you encounter a rattlesnake napping in the shade, the chances are he won't move when you walk by him, unless you approach him directly. However, they warm up when they are in the light, and that makes them agile enough to do what they have to do. Many animals are physically strengthened by light. I believe we humans are as well.

Again, the Bible teaches that the serpent is subtler than any creature God has made. By observing the way of Snakes in their natural habitat we can learn *much* about our spiritual adversary. The Devil has been labeled as a serpent since the very beginning (Revelation 12:9).

You should recall that he appeared in the form of a serpent to Adam and Eve in the Garden of Eden. He may take on any form he desires, which is something we should be constantly aware of. He can deceive us into thinking that he is an angel of light (2nd Corinthians 11:14), who many times makes it difficult for us to discern good from evil. Do not underestimate his subtlety nor his great power.

Wild Donkeys

Ever encounter a wild Donkey or wild Burro? There are a few out here in the wilderness, but a lot more wander the desert terrain in and around Death Valley. If you're camping out there you can usually hear one braying off in the distance. Sometimes they'll wander right into your camp, but for the most part they're skittish. They move quickly too. You most likely won't get a rope on one of them.

However, if your rope toss is successful, you had better be prepared to get dragged through the desert brush. It's best to leave them alone—best to just watch them, perhaps toss them a carrot or two, and enjoy their company. They'll usually hang around awhile and investigate you, then wander off peacefully.

Donkeys have never been considered among the elite animals. They don't carry great warriors into battle. They never pulled fancy chariots in the days of the Pharaohs. Yet, they are quite dependable and almost tireless beasts, capable of carrying heavier packs than horses quite a bit further than horses. Pack stations frequently use them nowadays to carry visitors' gear into recreational wilderness areas. Trail crews nationwide use them to haul trail-building materials and equipment. At Grand Canyon they carry hundreds of annual visitors along steep, hair-raising trails into its breathtaking depths on a daily basis.

In the early days of our American West, around 1873, a fellow by the name of W.T. Coleman built the first Borax works in Death Valley. He developed the famous system of 20 mule-team wagons that hauled the processed mineral 165 miles across that arid desert to the railroad at Mojave. The place where he originally mined is just a ghost town now. I might add here that there are a few ghost town remnants in Death Valley. It's a very interesting place to explore if you are a ghost town enthusiast.

The point is, the folk's who moved away from there left *everything* behind, including the mules—mostly Donkeys and Burros. Over the last 130 years or so those animals have roamed wild and have continued to breed. I find it exciting to see these wild and beautiful creatures wandering among the desert plants. I especially love to hear them bray. Burros are peaceful animals. Like I mentioned before, in ancient times no great warriors climbed aboard Donkeys. Most warriors were all accomplished horsemen. But in the ancient Near East, both kings and princes rode on Donkeys. The difference between the two (horseman and Donkey rider) was related to the prevalent events in the land they occupied.

A horse-riding king was a *warrior*, while a Donkey-riding *ruler* surveyed a peaceful land from his saddle. A warrior would meet out justice with a sword. A ruler pronounced justice with his words. What I am getting at is that Jesus, the King of Kings, announced his authority from the back of a young Donkey (Matthew 21:1-11). He was indeed a *ruler.* Great multitudes of people came to honor this Ruler of Rulers as He rode into Jerusalem on the back of a common Donkey.

He was not a warrior who came to fight our physical battles. He came in peace as a servant King. He came to display a servant's heart and to set an example for us, so that we might learn to depend upon Him and allow Him to express this attitude through our own hearts. He performed many miracles, which proved who He was and where He was from. The thrust of His teaching was that all would come to know Him and His Father as being humble and lowly in heart.

Yet, no one knew Him, even though He had been spoken of in many ways and identified repeatedly as the Messiah (*anointed one of God*) throughout the ancient Scriptures, which teachings the religious leaders of those days were supposedly knowledgeable of. When He finally entered Jerusalem aboard that lowly Donkey, with multitudes of supporters in His train, the religious leaders along with the whole of the city, whom he had ministered to time and again for more than three years, were stirred, and asked, "Who is this?"

Many still ask that question. All *should have known* who He was. A few did, but lacked the courage to stand with Him to the end. Personally, I continue to learn to know Him. Much of my learning comes through a study of the things He has made. So, when I see a wild Donkey out here, that most glorious beast of burden, it brings these things I've just talked to you about into my remembrance. The teacher is no better than the pupil. It's always good to be re-reminded and made *aware* of the things that truly pertain to this life. After all, we live in a world that is pretty much unaware, do we not?

The Way of the Eagle

Does the eagle mount up at your command and make its nest on high? (Job 39:27 NKJV)

I've spotted Eagles at different times while on my hikes along these various trails, both in the deserts and in the mountains. Perhaps we'll have the good fortune to catch a glimpse of one today. I was hiking along Rush Creek near June Lake in the eastern Sierra Nevada a few summers back. It was there in a somewhat remote and picturesque area of the high country that I had a most unique encounter with a *Golden Eagle*.

The Greek word for Eagle is *aetos*, which means, to blow as the wind or become one with the wind. The Psalms teach us that the way of an eagle in flight is too wonderful to understand (Psalm 30:18,19). I had just rounded a bend in the trail when I saw the Golden. She was soaring at eye level, above the canyon, just about 30 feet west of where I was journeying along the high trail.

It was a very large Eagle, so I judged her to be female. She was incredibly close to me. She slowed, almost stopping in mid-air. She was riding the wind, correcting for every deviation of its velocity, all the while seemingly investigating me. She was looking right at me! At one point I believe, or at least would like to believe, that our eyes actually met. It's hard to tell if they're looking directly into your eyes, but just having the Eagle behold me was an honor in itself.

I didn't move a muscle or even twitch a finger. I was thinking, 'the good Lord has indeed blessed me in allowing me to witness such a grand and glorious wonder so close at hand. I am indeed humbled by His kindness!' I was suspended in time, hopeful that the encounter might last a little while longer. I was overwhelmed at the Eagle's control—fascinated by it.

Then, in a moment, in the twinkling of an eye she dipped a wing and turned off, headed down along the canyon to pick up speed. I estimated that she was flying somewhere between 50 and 60 miles per hour. I soon caught her in my binoculars and tracked her until she was out of sight. How majestic and graceful she was!

I've known Eagles to attain speeds in excess of 100 miles per hour while in a dive. They can hold those speeds while maintaining focus on the object at which they are diving. They are so well coordinated they can avoid in flight collisions at that speed and can actually drag just a fraction of an inch of talon across the back of another bird, sending it spiraling to the ground in complete shock. I've seen them close their talons, as if making a fist, to strike their prey as they swoop on by. Pilots have reported seeing Golden Eagles in flight above fifteen thousand feet.

Eagles have tremendous vision. You and I, according to medical science, have some two hundred thousand of what they call *visual receptors*, per square centimeter, within our eyes. The Eagle has 1.6 million receptors per square centimeter; eight times that of a human. That makes for an extremely high visual resolution or 'optical clarity', in simpler wording. Let me illustrate:

Imagine sitting in the very last row of the Dallas stadium during football season—I mean who can afford closer seats, right? With a pair of binoculars I might be able to catch the main action of the game. From that same distance an Eagle can individualize every blade of grass on the playing field. An Eagle could read three-inch letters on a billboard one mile away.

They can see small fish jumping out of the water five miles out to sea. They can spot fish in a swiftly flowing stream from thousands of feet in the air. They have remarkable vitality. An Eagle weighing about twenty pounds has enough strength in its talons to break both of the bones in a man's forearm, just by grasping it firmly. Any small, unsuspecting prey would be crushed instantly under that kind of power.

If you recall, I had an operation on my stomach a few years back. I learned something about the Eagle's talons from my surgeon, after he had stitched me up. He informed me that surgical needles were modeled after Eagle's talons. They are specially crafted to pierce the flesh and not to tear it. I was thankful to the Lord that day for His unique design of the Eagle's talons, and for the both informed and skillful surgeon who knew how to use that particularly well-designed needle.

When an Eagle soars it is not by his or her own strength. They effectively extend their great wings and are lifted by the rising currents of air. They just simply make themselves *available to the wind*. I too can soar within my own spirit like the Eagle, when I make myself *available to God and yield to His Spirit*. I have soared many times while just thinking about His greatness. I have danced atop desert mesas and high mountain peaks.

I see His greatness and feel His presence in all of His wonders. I feel it with each breath that I take along these hiking trails. I can also reach out and touch a variety of His different works at any time. This particular uplifting of spirit has been identified as the *Rocky Mountain High* by a songwriter, but it is much more than that. I feel kindred to the Eagle in this way.

The Eagle—a brilliant creature, extraordinarily graceful, with incomprehensible control, incredible speed, supreme vision and commanding strength. It's no wonder then that God pays grand tribute to their majesty. How well I have learned through my own experiences the immeasurable value of the following Biblical teaching:

Do you not know? Have you not heard? The Lord is the everlasting God, the Creator of the ends of the earth. He will not grow tired or weary, and His understanding no one can fathom. He gives strength to the weary, and increases the power of the weak. Even youths grow tired and weary, and young men stumble and fall; but those who hope in the Lord will renew their strength. They will soar (mount up) *on wings like eagles; they will run and not grow weary, they will walk and not be faint.* (Isaiah 40:28-31 NIV)

*

We've so much to learn from the creatures God has made—from Coyotes, from Jack Rabbits, from Locusts, from Owls, from Sheep, from Ravens, from Snakes, from wild Donkeys and from the Eagle. Actually, from every single solitary creature God has created upon the earth—insects, birds, reptiles, mammals, fish, you name it.

There is not one creature alive on the earth or in the sea that God has not individually, diversely and uniquely designed for a specific purpose. According to the Scriptures, each one of them could indeed *wisely* educate us. The Scriptures teach us that each and every one of them knows, honors and trusts in God, their creator (Job 12:7-10).

102

Being the highest order of creation on God's earth, shouldn't we humans all the more do likewise? Modern science has learned much about the habits and life-style of many of the earth's creatures. There are huge libraries stocked full of this particular type of information throughout the world. The problem however with modern science, and with most textbooks on the inhabitants of the creation, is that they fall short by failing to *recognize God* as the author of all things (Genesis 1:20-26).

Therefore, the best of the presently existing theories, reasoning's or arrived conclusions of mankind regarding the creatures of the earth are burdened with false or misleading information. In other words, you can't really trust them for complete accuracy. They represent no understanding of true origins and only scratch on the surface of understanding the qualities and abilities of any of these creatures. Discernment that considers God's time, perception, direction and purposes pertaining to what He has made is what's required at the highest level.

The Biblical book of Job, chapters 37 through 42, is a great place for the whole world to begin. Secular textbooks are useful, providing that you consider the information and apply it under the *proper light*, which is God's truth and eternal purpose. Most rewarding of course is your own personal observation of God's creatures in their natural environment. Your spirit will soar as you watch and contemplate the creature creations first hand, while you carefully and thankfully consider God's words:

Ask the animals, and they will teach you, or the birds of the air and they will tell you; or speak to the earth, and it will teach you, or let the fish of the sea inform you. Which of these does not know that the hand of the Lord has done this? In his hand is the life of every creature and the breath of all mankind (Job 12:7-10 NIV).

A sad note here: There's talk now that there are too many buffalo in the American west, and hunting is now permitted in some regions. The wolves also are endangered in this regard, around the world, because they think there are too many of them as well. They are now capturing the pups and actually shooting them in the heads at point blank range. People who can do something like this—God forgive me—deserve similar treatment.

Just recently, a group of employees from the Department of Agriculture (college educated) were fearful that there were too many starlings flying around in the New England states…So, they threw poisoned seed into their feeding areas. A few days later, the birds were dropping out of the sky by the hundreds—on the roadway, in peoples yards, in front of businesses, and into the local water supplies.

Do you think these things grieve the Lord in His heart? It all boils down to what you feel about Him—what you've learned about Him from the very start of your hike on the *Trail of Truth*. What He has to endure for the sake of His chosen is unfathomable! The very next time you're out on the trail, consider the birds and animals. Watch them and learn from them. Talk to them. You *can* get their attention.

Many of them have not had the English language spoken at them, and most of them are fearful because humans many times hunt them. Their families may have been the victims of gunfire, and so they hesitate in trusting us. Some are dangerous because of this mistrust. It's best to stand still and speak gently. Do not approach them suddenly. If you're not inclined to stop and talk, then at least give them the courtesy of a "good morning" as you hike on by them. Move slowly in hope that you will not frighten them.

If you are a pet owner and in the habit of taking your pet for a walk or along with you on your hike, slow down a little bit and let that particular creature soak up the Creation. Let them wander around and investigate things. They like to sniff the grass, flowers, trees and brush. God gave them a great sense of smell, acute hearing and good eyesight, that they might enjoy His creation.

They are indeed aware of these gifts and are also aware of their source. Allow them to appreciate their surroundings in their own way. If you're in a hurry, don't take them with you. If they're on a leash, don't jerk on it in your impatience. How would you like someone to throw a rope around your neck and jerk on it? What goes around comes around.

Your concern for God's creatures honors their Creator. Therefore, do not intentionally crush the smaller species; the ants, the beetles, or any of the crawling things. Having a merciful and generous relationship with God's creatures will indeed draw you closer to Him. And by your standard of measure (the degree of your kindness) it shall be measured to you, and more shall be given you besides (Mark 4:24).

Again, the creatures know instinctively who God is, and they know much more about Him than you do, so remain humble in their presence. Animals are just one of the reasons we humans are without excuse for not knowing that God exists. The Scripture on the front title page of this book bears that out. The entire creation cries out to you. That's what this writing is all about. Pay attention, for it will be both life and health to you.

Chapter Five...Trail's End
The Mountain of Believing

You're not supposed to read the last chapter first. That would be like reading the final book of the Bible before you read the other 65 books—a grievous mistake. It is true that the mystery surrounding the prophetic book of Revelation, the Bible's final writing, draws attention to it, yet hundreds of authors who have written on it (expressing a variety of opinions) have been unable to interpret it correctly. Many of them have never read any other portions of the Bible.

So it is with this book—you will not deal rightly with this last chapter until you have read with much attention the first 4 chapters, nor will you comprehend its most important teaching. If you are one of those attempting to read this last chapter first—hoping to discover something about this book—looking for a reason to either reject it or to consider it—then you are indeed chasing after the wind.

That's like being airlifted onto a high mountaintop and foregoing the exhilaration and illumination of a challenging hiking experience. If you are not one of those attempting to read this last chapter first, then I commend you on your wisdom and integrity, and I apologize for this brief but necessary delay in the chapter's opening.

I thought I would conclude this writing with a hike up the Mountain of Believing. I realize that we have hiked a long way together, but in learning about God enlightenment never ends. The trailhead is just south of the Desert Trail; in fact it begins just where the Desert Trail ends. It's a good hike for you—I think a needed one, so take some refreshment and then we'll start the climb. We will consider the Mountain of Believing from four elevations—Base Camp, the Early Ascent, the North Face (rock of promises) and the Summit Ridge...

 ### *Base Camp*

The *Mountain of Believing* is a no-nonsense climb. True belief itself is an exceedingly high mountain that must be climbed from Base Camp. Let's talk about this that you might better understand what I am saying and where I am going. Actually, believing in God is a *gift*. As a gift freely given to you, your personal belief in God now becomes a matter of your own maturity into understanding (Hebrews 6:1-3). You have been given a gift and you have to work with it.

Since we are incapable of spiritually believing without God's gift, it is obvious that the understanding involved with this gift and concerning this gift requires intensive training and an unlimited amount of time—perhaps a lifetime. The *emotion* of initial belief that God exists, that He is real, is only ground level or *Base Camp* belief. God requires that we grow with our gift—that we mature in our faith. We must therefore climb a high and difficult mountain toward spiritual maturity from Base Camp.

The Mountain of Believing itself is steep. The ascent trail to spiritual maturity is narrow and there are numerous places along that trail where climbers have stopped to rest—places where many remain resting, not able to or not wanting to continue the arduous journey. Their faith is limited—sometimes misguided, hindering their belief, and as a result true *spiritual maturity* cannot take place within them. Bottom line; they have not realized the extreme value of their gift.

A growing Christian—one increasing in faith and belief—will encounter many people like this at these resting places as he or she continues on their upward journey. Maneuvering around them on the narrow trail can sometimes be difficult, but never impossible. Here are some of the difficulties you, as a true believer, may encounter:

There are a myriad of beliefs out there in the world. There is however, in spite of world opinion, only *one* true God, who is extraordinarily revealed in nature and Scripture through three distinct personalities. These are the Father, the Son, and the Holy Spirit (Matthew 28:19). There is also only *one* way, according to Scripture (which is God's *only* written revelation to us), to approach this Godhead…

Jesus has said: *"I am the way, the truth and the life. No one comes to the Father except through Me."* Yet, He also said; *"No one can come to Me unless the Father who sent Me draws him.*

Everyone who listens to the Father and learns from Him comes to Me." In addition, the apostle Paul said, "*No one can say that Jesus is Lord, except by the Holy Spirit.*" He also said, "*If we are led by the Spirit of God, then we are the children of God.*" [1]

First of all we can know, according to the word of God, that no one, no matter what his or her ideas, philosophy, religious belief or personal background, can come to God *except through Jesus Christ*. That overrules the vain attempts of *many* people involved in/with various world religions, who think they know how to approach the God of the universe. Secondly, no one can come to Jesus unless he or she is *drawn* to Him by the mercy of God the Father. Again, belief is indeed a gift.

Thirdly, everyone who *truly* learns from the Father *comes to Jesus*. Fourthly, no one can claim that Jesus is Lord, except *through the Holy Spirit*. And finally, only if we are led by the *Spirit of God* can we claim to be the *children of God*. Any world religion or philosophy or idea that teaches anything other than what I have just outlined for you here is obviously a false and vain religion or philosophy or idea, and rightly, according to Scripture, should be considered as such.

Coming to God and believing in Jesus is *unquestionably* a matter of God *allowing* it to be so (Ephesians 2:8). Once again, believing in God is a *gift. True belief* in God then becomes an *individual honor* that for reasons only God knows is not given to every creature (Romans 9:15). You must learn to treat it as such. If you are a *true believer*, you must endeavor to learn the value of such good fortune in your life. You have indeed a most precious gift—you are in fact chosen of God (Ephesians 1:4).

Near the Mountain of Believing you will find many so-called believers who have no concept of what you have just learned. A little further up, at *Base Camp* itself, you will find many new believers who know there is only one God. They are not necessarily short-time believers. Many there have believed in God for a long period of time, but their faith and belief have not matured. They haven't understood their *need* to climb further up the mountain. They remain at Base Camp where they can and do encourage new arrivals, yet their own personal desire may be to not continue any further.

They often *feel* that they *do not need* to precede any further. Unfortunately they have not realized the true *in-depth value* of their gift. They are, shall we say, 'content' at their particular state of belief. The reasons for their contentment vary and many camping there are not necessarily 'honestly' content. Some are content with the basic concepts of salvation:

They have believed and have been baptized into Christ, but no longer continue to study the Bible and learn about their Lord and His individual purpose for them. Many others there have also believed in Jesus but have not yet been baptized, and so the Spirit of God does not dwell within them (Acts 2:38). Personal feelings, no matter how strong, *do not* confirm the indwelling of the Spirit of God. Only the Word can justify the presence of the Holy Spirit. Many Biblical passages confirm this truth.

In the meantime, there are also some truly converted Christians at Base Camp who have not started up the mountain because of their fear of leaving the world behind. They hold to the philosophies and scientific teachings of the world and do not totally accept the truths of God. Their level of belief is indeed a 'Base Camp' level. There are non-baptized believers who have actually ascended to higher levels on the mountain than true believers because they desire to continue their learning.

Although these individuals are unaware that they are not truly Christians by *obedience to the faith* (Acts 5:32), each one *can* mature somewhat by applying Biblical principles to their life —no doubt about it. They are however limited as to the distance they can ascend on the Mountain of Believing. Not having laid a true foundation at Base Camp, much of their understanding or misunderstanding is based on the trickery and deceit of Satan. They continue to learn, but never come to the knowledge of the *truth* (2nd Timothy 3:7).

They are not against Christianity, but they lack the knowledge of the most vital elementary doctrines of its teachings. In time they can become hardened in their own personal beliefs, thus failing to understand their need to renew their minds and become like little children (Romans 12:2 & Matthew 18:2-4). They also lack the ability to *purely* influence new believers, causing many to continue to live in error of the truth.

The point of this entire writing is for you to learn and to understand that the *strength of your belief* in God requires a *firm foundation* of *truth*, and a *continued ascent* in your *learning*—an ascent on the *Mountain of Believing*. The more you learn of God through experience in understanding *truth*, the stronger and more effective your respect and belief in Him and His care for you will become. Sincere belief, from a heart that is guided by the Spirit of God and not the popular teachings of men, is given a most profound guarantee of success (John 15:7,8).

Your prayer life will improve. Your ability to understand your own needs and the more important needs of others will become exceedingly more evident. Your ability to understand the Scriptures and bring them to life will embrace your heart and mind. Life will take on *new meaning* and an *ever-increasing hope*. The peace that passes all understanding can be available to you. Let those of you then whose desire is truth courageously depart from *Base Camp*, open your hearts and minds, and begin an illuminating ascent with me on the *Mountain of Believing*...

The Early Ascent

If you have been given the gift of belief and you have left Base Camp and begun your ascent on the Mountain of Believing, then you are embarking on an incredibly eye-opening, thought provoking, life changing journey. As you ascend on to *spiritual maturity* you will begin to leave the world's concepts behind and below you. The basic philosophies and false scientific teachings and beliefs of the world do not compare in any way with the truths of God, yet they make it extremely difficult for the truth to be taught and understood.

For instance, the age of the earth, along with the formation of mountains, rivers and canyons, is completely misunderstood by most modern scientists and hundreds of thousands to millions of believers. But, the accurate knowledge of these things should be basic or indeed in the process of becoming basic to the true believer. I am going to give you a few examples of some *basic truths* that you will need to learn to believe in *before* you get too far up from Base Camp.

Without these understandings your further ascent on the mountain will be indeed slow going, difficult, and eventually impossible. First and foremost is the understanding that God's only written revelation to us (the Bible) is *absolute* truth, and *anything* that disagrees with it can only be interpreted as being misrepresented, misunderstood, misleading, or false. If you have progressed to *this point* of understanding, which does take some study time and experienced reasoning, you should then as a believer have a *firm grip* on the following truths:

1) The Lord formed the heavens we can see and the present earth upon which we live, with all of its full-grown plants, fish, birds and animals, in six (6) literal 24-hour days as we know them from our earthly frame of reference. He also made the planets and the stars and the sun and the moon to give light upon the earth. All of these creations are in perfect order, according to His plan.

All things of nature including plants, animals, birds and insects upon the earth as well as the creatures of the sea remain in perfect harmony, depending upon one another for continued existence. *All things point to a supreme intelligence as creator. True scientists tell us that if one studies the physical sciences long enough and hard enough, he/she is *forced* to come to the aforementioned* conclusion. True belief looks *confidently* beyond the teachings of men.

2) On the sixth day of creation, from the dust of the earth, the Lord made man in His own *image* (a spirit being with creative abilities). He made a woman from the rib of this man, Adam, who was to be his helper and his equal. She was called Eve (*mother of all living*), and together they became the original ancestors of the entire world's human population. Unfortunately the couple fell from God's grace by giving into temptation, and were a part of the sad event that brought depravity, decay, disease and death upon the earth.

3) This present earth from the time of its habitable formation is less than 7000 years old. 1656 years after our earth's creation (around 5000 years ago), the Lord brought an overwhelming flood of waters upon a greatly populated earth, which destroyed all mankind, save 8 souls who were aboard an ark, and which reshaped the entire earth, resulting in the geography that currently exists. Many plant and animal species and sea creatures were buried into extinction during that cataclysmic flood, which accounts for present day coal and oil deposits as well as the fossil record.

Selected animals and birds aboard the ark are the ancestors of today's various species worldwide. From the surviving family of Noah and his descendants the people also began to multiply. They were eventually divided by language and race (through divine miracle at the tower of Babel) and continued to move about, populating areas of the entire earth. This post-flood population is still growing. Since everyone descends from the family of Noah, we need to realize that this relationship leaves us with the duty to respect, to honor and to care for one another—worldwide.

4) Since Satan is the ruler of this world (Matthew 4:8,9 & John 12:31), you cannot therefore trust in the wisdom, *nor* in the philosophies, *nor* in the majority of the educational systems of the various kingdoms in this present world. The world's population for the most part does not know their place on the earth, rejects the authority of God, and is ignorant concerning His attributes. They are inconsiderate of His sovereignty. Therefore, the wisdom of the world is mere foolishness in His sight (1st Corinthians 3:19). God is in control of earthly events and will eventually allow this present earth to be destroyed by fire, but will bring forth a new earth where only goodness dwells (2nd Peter 3:10-13).

5) Following the life-giving attitudes of a man called *Jesus*, the Son of God, is the only way of true wisdom and life for the entire believing world. No one anywhere in the world can come to God the Father, regardless of his or her beliefs, except through a belief in and submission to the saving will of Jesus Christ (John 14:6). It was His ultimate sacrifice on a Roman cross that paid the sin debt for the entire world (1st John 2:2). All peoples of the world are under the curse of sin and Jesus is their only hope of redemption from it (Romans 3:23,24).

Fact: If you doubt any of the five truths I have listed above (a very small list I might add), please don't take offense, but you are just not yet a *true* believer in God. If you cling to the false sciences, deceptive philosophies or vain religions or traditions of the world and call yourself a believer in God, then you are unfortunately only deceiving yourself. I'm not trying to be hard on you here, but your life is passing away and your need is to develop an eternal attitude—to become a *mature* believer. For if in this life only we have hope in Christ, we are of all people the most pitiable (Philippians 2:5, 1ˢᵗ Corinthians 15:19).

The Early Ascent from Base Camp requires that you acknowledge *who God is*, and that you trust in *what He has proclaimed* and *not* in the concepts, theories and conclusions of unknowing or unbelieving men and women of the world. Know that the 'knowledge' (wisdom) of mankind within this world is pure foolishness to God. If you want to increase in faith and belief, then you must courageously turn from the world in your thinking and follow the truths of God. You must be *transformed* by the *renewing of your mind* (Romans 12:2).

You may, at first, find truth difficult to follow since you were educated by the world. All of us have been educated by the world. Its affect in many cases is similar to 'brainwashing.' This may seem a harsh term, but *keep in mind* that God has said that Satan *is* the ruler of this world, that this present world is fading away, that it will be destroyed, and that *truth* will be all that remains (2nd Peter 3:10). Renewing your mind with what is true and right and everlasting and then acting positively on those realizations is the *only* thing that will save you or anyone else.

*It's time now to ask yourself; have you truly begun the Early Ascent from Base Camp? Without learning to accept and learning to trust in the five minimum understandings I presented to you, you will be unable to grow properly in your faith and unable to climb any higher *spiritually* on the Mountain of Believing. But, know that belief in the *truths* of God can indeed set you free, that you might indeed benefit from your climb. Jesus Himself said, "*If you abide in My word, you are My* *disciples indeed. And you shall know the truth, and the truth shall make you free"* (John 8:31, 32 NKJV).

In this world we are indeed slaves—slaves to the world's teachings and slaves to the consequences of those teachings upon and within our earthly lives. But in Christ and in His *truth* we are made free—free to embark on *learning* the truth, free to reject the teachings of men, free from the condemning judgment of God, and spiritually free to live our earthly lives until the end, learning from God alone, trusting in God alone, serving others through God alone and looking forward to *eternal life*. What unparalleled *assurance* we have in trusting our Creator! Do not therefore be deceived through trusting in yourself (Proverbs 3:5,6).

The North Face (rock of promises)

If we have overcome our fears of doubt regarding the Bible itself and we know that it is true, and if we have courageously disregarded the concepts, theories and error-filled conclusions of false science, it is now that our Early Ascent from Base Camp is complete. It is time to climb on *toward more mature understanding*. It is time to approach the North Face, which I call *the rock of promises*, so named because our entire Christian experience; birth, initial growth, maturity, ultimate salvation and eternal life, is based *entirely* on God's *promises* (2nd Peter 1:3,4).

I'm going to repeat that thought by saying that every step we take in life trusting in God is based 'one-hundred (100) percent' on His promises. However, even though we've come this far up the mountain through believing and acting *on* those promises, the chances of us *turning back* to our former thoughts and ideas can become much greater. Our trust in God can be thwarted. Satan wages a constant battle within us and around us to turn us from God. The more knowledge, faith and belief we accumulate, all the more fiercely he fights against us to produce apprehension or doubt.

"For we are not fighting against people made of flesh and blood, but against the evil rulers and authorities of the unseen world, against those mighty powers of darkness who rule this world, and against wicked spirits in the heavenly realms." (Ephesians 6:12 NLT)

Satan does not want you to learn anything or believe anything that will be detrimental to his hopeful reign over your personal life. He is the prince and ruler of this world. He will accuse you for the remainder of your earthly life, while God will continue to test your faith—to purify you as choice silver. Therefore, difficulties in your life *will* increase. Some believe that God will not send as many difficulties your way once you become a Christian. God never sends difficulties your way, but Satan does. He will endeavor to make your life extremely miserable after your conversion. Before that he could care less.

Since your ideas toward the world have now changed considerably, you are going to lose the confidence of some close relatives, perhaps even those within your own household. You may also lose the close friendship you have with some of your associates. In addition, the further up the mountain you climb, the fewer true believers you will encounter, for *narrow is the road that leads to life, and only a few ever find it*. Bottom line— the Christian path of life is extremely difficult on this earth. The end rewards however will be exceedingly great.[2]

The most difficult portion of your climb up the Mountain of Believing comes when you reach what I am calling the North

Face or *the rock of promises*. You will reach the foot of this area when you have climbed over the aforementioned rocks and obstacles we have encountered since we arrived at Base Camp. You have believed in many of God's teachings and promises thus far or you wouldn't be where we are now. Yet, this particular face of the mountain, the *rock of promises*, is even more difficult to ascend.

It has been a foot trail so far, but now you are going to need both your hands and feet, some ropes and lots of *courage, faith* and *hope*—the no-nonsense stuff. Due to the *immeasurable* weakness of human nature—our natural heart and mind—many of God's promises seem notably difficult to comprehend and to hold on to. But remember, we count on His promises through *faith, not by sight* (2nd Corinthians 5:7). We move ahead, not always sure where we're going—but we have to get going—trusting in Him. When the north wind wails along the face of the mountain and threatens your foothold here you must struggle against it and continue your climb.

While ascending a steep, rock face as the rock of promises is, I would like you to imagine that there are several *pitons* hammered into the face of the rock at various intervals along the ascent. Climbers' pitons are wedged shaped for hammering into small cracks in the rock. The outer end of the piton is usually in the shape of a ring or hook, for securing your carabiners (self-locking rope holders, similar to D-rings) as you make the climb. Once pitons are hammered into place they usually remain in the rock for use by future climbers.

We're going to imagine the piton placements as the individual promises of God, which you are learning to trust in on your ascent up the Mountain of Believing. Each piton represents a different promise that you must ascend to, hang onto with your rope, understand *or* accept, and then continue on up from. Do you have a mental picture? Great! You will have a great distance to climb up this rock of promises before reaching the backbone —the ridge of faith that ascends toward the summit. I hope that your climbing gear is in good shape for this North Face ascent.

When you first became a Christian through being water baptized into Christ, the Bible teaches us that your past sins were forgiven—washed away by the living Word of God, through the death of Christ (Romans 6:3). When you arose from that watery grave the Bible also teaches that the Spirit of God entered your life (Acts 2:38). These promises of *forgiveness of sins* and the *gift of the Holy Spirit*, I believe, are the greatest of God's promises in the entire Bible. And because they are so great, sometimes we humans have difficulty in believing that these *promises* are actually true—we all encounter times of 'spiritual weakness.'

One reason for this is that, after baptism, we are still *capable of sin* and still continue to do so, even after we have been given the *promise* of a new life! Our *nature* to sin does not change through baptism, only our *position* with God changes. We still sin and if we say that we do not sin, we only prove ourselves to be liars. However, though we continue to unwillingly sin, the blood of Christ faithfully and justly cleanses us from all unrighteousness as we confess our sins and pray through the intersession of the Holy Spirit, who helps us in our weaknesses to walk in God's way; having the intersession of Jesus on our behalf.[4]

These are *promises*—we won't 'feel' them happening, we just have to count on them as truth. Another reason we may doubt the promise of forgiveness is the fact that we may bear lasting *consequences* from our past sins—consequences that war violently against our ability to accept forgiveness. The consequences of sin are unrelenting. Contrary to popular belief forgiveness does not remove consequences, but only allows us to *accept them*.

We cannot bring back the person we murdered. We cannot bring back the wife and children we deserted through adultery. We cannot get out of prison for the robbery we committed. We cannot return to the job we were fired from. We usually cannot undo the words we spoke in anger or the damage we committed through rage. We usually cannot win back the hearts of those we've hurt or lost through our sin(s) along life's journey.

In other words, the consequences of our sins will continue, whatever they are, even though God has forgiven us of the sins themselves, for God has *promised, "Do not be deceived, God is not mocked; for whatever a man sows, that will he also reap"* (Galatians 6:7 NKJV). Consequences can totally break the spirit of a man or a woman. Life can become painfully unbearable for the forgiven sinner, due to the *unforgiving consequences* of sin. All the suicides that have *ever* been committed throughout the world are the direct result of an inability to bear the consequences of sin in one form or another, no if's, and's or but's about it.

A third reason we may doubt the promise of forgiveness is that other people usually don't truly forgive us the way God does. God forgives us, totally removing our sins, even from His memory! People usually don't forgive us to that extent. Somebody will always continue to point the finger at you. Someone will always be there to put you on a guilt trip. Fortunately, God doesn't think like people do. His ways are far above our ways, as are His thoughts, His intentions and His judgments. No one can know His mind or be His counselor.[3] The fact remains that His compassion never ends. He forgives us of our sins. His mercy is new *every* morning (Lamentations 3:22-24).

I believe the forth reason I'm going to give you here is the most profound. We cannot grasp an understanding of God's true and everlasting forgiveness of sin because we *cannot forgive ourselves*. I have searched the Scriptures for many years, but have not found an example of anyone who could honestly forgive themselves. I heard a renowned man once say that it was an impossible thing to do. So far, I agree with him. I believe with all of my heart that we can *learn to accept* the *consequences* of sin, but I don't believe we can ever completely forgive ourselves for the sin(s)—not if our spirits have truly been broken and our hearts remain contrite.

On the other hand, some people use the crutch, "Well, I'm only human." Though that is true, it will not remove the scars from the heart, nor from those hearts scared through our sin. These crutch-walkers have not *truly acknowledged* their sins. Jesus died a horrible death for our sins. He bears our scars as well. How can anyone forgive himself or herself for that? However, what the inability to forgive ourselves should accomplish is to allow us to see our need to serve God more willingly and fervently—for those who have much to be forgiven of will in turn love much, and those who have little to be forgiven of will love little (Luke 7:47).

I have learned that personal pain develops humility. Though the pain of my former sins mentally cripple me, I would not have learned how to depend upon God without that pain, nor would I ever come to understand the depth and utter depravity of my sins and the irreversible damage they have caused. I would not be able to fathom any part of the crucifixion of Jesus. It is the guilt of sin, the pain of sin, the remorse of sin and the consequences of sin that teach me who and what I really am. That makes the *joy* of God's forgiveness exceedingly joyful! This joy is a most humbling experience to the truly remorseful.

It is this deep anguish within my soul that serves to bring change to my heart of stone, produce healing in my soul, and build character through the Spirit of God working within me. That particular anguish of deep repentance was one of the reasons King David was called, by God Himself, *a man after My own heart* (Acts 13:22). Consequences are indeed tough to live with. The piton then which represents God's forgiveness, this very first on the rock of promises, is indeed a difficult one to climb on past, is it not? Actually, it all depends.

It all depends on your attitude. The problem is, if you do not get past it you're going to be stuck right here on the North Face. You will not be able to climb any higher on this rock of promises. You will be unable to explore the magnitude or depth of any other of God's precious promises. There are indeed many enriching promises on ahead of you, so you need to get above this piton by learning to accept who you are, what you are, and how God deals with your sins. He forgives them—doesn't hold them against you. You need to deal with them as well—to consider your failures as stepping-stones to maturity. God knows your remorse, and loves you exceedingly for it (Psalm 51:17).

You need to take a new grip with those tired hands and take a firm hold on your climbing rope, so that you won't fall back and hurt yourself. Now, straighten out those shaky legs—accept your failures as growing pains and climb on up—get past that piton. This may take some time and that's not really a problem. The key is in *knowing* where you are on the rock of promises, *acknowledging* where you are, and then having the patience to *remain* where you are until you have acquired the wisdom, knowledge, skill and courage to proceed upward. This particular process is simply a further development of humility.

This patience will result in an illuminating increase of understanding, faith and belief in your Christian journey. That particular illumination is the revelation of your growing dependence upon God, for you are *slowly learning* that without Him you can do *absolutely nothing* (John 15:5). Embrace that attitude, because few ever really comprehend their need for it— by the time they do their life is gone. The poor and the destitute are the lucky ones here. They hold the secrets of depending upon God. They know the way to priceless treasures, and their journey is most difficult. (Luke 6:20)

God has indeed given us many *exceedingly great and precious promises,* through which we gain the hope needed to continue this earthly life's journey. Among those most familiar to Bible students are His shelter through life's many storms, answered prayer, His watchful eye in maintaining our path, His helping hand during illness or death, His bountiful love, mercy and forgiveness, along with food, clothing and relief of worries and cares—actually everything that concerns us, including an inner peace that passes all understanding—and in the end, eternal life!

He has promised us vast, new heavens and a new earth, with unending peace among its inhabitants. I believe that this new world will be where our most precious dreams come true. These promises we've considered here are all found within God's written word, the Bible. Each of these promises requires *distinct elevations of understanding* on our part, just as ascending to another piton on the North Face requires a distinct movement—a calculated movement.

However, unlike the piton ascent, these levels of understanding are spiritual levels and not physical levels. We attain to these spiritual elevations of understanding *only* through our continued faith and trust in God—our continued ascent on the *rock* of *His promises*. He is holding the climbing rope that we cling to. It is true that our belief in these promises usually requires faith in things that are not necessarily seen. Yet, if we look at these unseen things *spiritually,* we *will* eventually be able to see them—to know them.

Traditionally, seeing has always been believing. After we ascend the rock of promises and climb onto the Summit Ridge there is in fact much that we will be enabled to see. Through the eyes of one humbled by their sins God gives true sight, opening their heart to understanding. His mercy then becomes their anchor (Psalm 25). When you do reach the Summit Ridge, know that you have been allowed a monumental accomplishment, and all the credit goes to your hiking partner—our Lord Jesus.

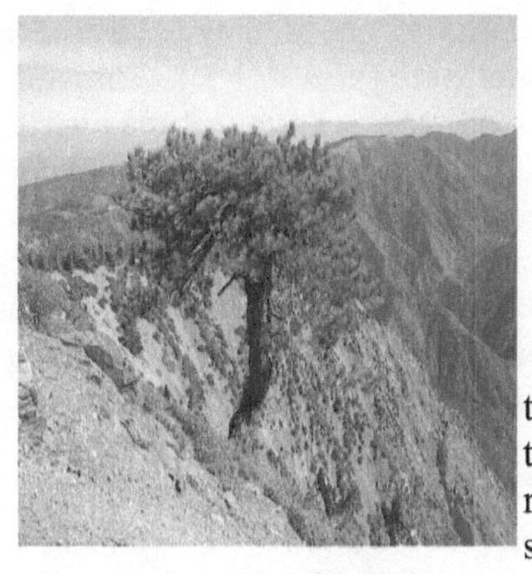

The Summit Ridge

The picture associated with this chapter (page 107) is that of the Devil's Backbone, a razorback ridge on the high summit trail of Mt. San Antonio (Old Baldy), the highest peak in southern California's San Gabriel mountain range. The Devil's Backbone is a hair-raiser, an extremely narrow trek across a steep ridge, yet it offers grand vistas of both the Lytle Creek drainage on the north and east, and San Antonio Canyon on the south. I nearly met with disaster here once but was saved by Dr. Mike Mucci, a fellow hiker, whose swift hand caught the frame of my backpack just as I had lost my footing.

I learned something that day about hiking on that spiny ridge —to place one foot directly in front of the other, and to carefully place my hiking boot on solid ground with each and every step. It is definitely a place that will heighten your awareness. We have the given means and ability to also heighten our spiritual awareness, through the things God has made and the faith which those things can generate. We can learn so very much through the visible things around us that can give us wondrous insight into the invisible things—see the supernatural through the natural. That's when our hiking boots are on solid ground.

The Scriptures tell us that from the time the world was created people have been able to behold the earth and sky and all that God has made. They can clearly see His invisible qualities—His eternal power and divine nature, and so they have no excuse whatsoever for not knowing God (Romans 1:20). The Summit Ridge is a place where correct, repeated Biblical reading, faith, belief and trust in God's promises mesh together with the creation, allowing you to see as you have never seen before.

The trek from Base Camp to the Early Ascent, to the Rock of Promises and on up to the Summit Ridge culminates in a foundation that cannot be shaken. From here you can learn to see the unseen at all times. This concept was profoundly revealed through the simple, everyday teachings of Jesus, the Son of God:

"Observe how the lilies of the field grow; they do not toil nor do they spin. Yet, I say to you that even Solomon, in all his glory, did not clothe himself like one of these. But, if God so arrays the grass of the field, which is alive today and tomorrow is thrown into the furnace, will He not much more do so for you, Oh men of little faith?" (Matthew 6: 28-30 NASB)

King Solomon to this day is by far the wisest man who ever lived on the face of the earth. His wealth and possessions also far exceeded those of the wealthiest men or kings upon the earth throughout his lifetime (1st Kings 3:12, 13). Yet, in all of his glory and splendor he was not arrayed (fashioned/adorned) as magnificently as a simple flower of the field. Have you ever examined up close the tiniest flower blooming in a field? From the Summit Ridge you can see vast fields of radiant flowers far below you, each one a little different.

You can see majestic mountains and diverse canyons formed by the hand of God. This is also the home of the big horn sheep, the owl, the hawk and the golden eagle. It is indeed an honor to view any of these creatures. The rocks, the trees and the varying plants of the surrounding terrain speak to you of the incomparable glory and wisdom of God in His creativity. Have you ever plucked just an ordinary blade of grass and examined it closely? The intricate design of water canals and matter in just a single blade is awe-inspiring!

How much more in unfathomable, detailed splendor then are all these wonders seen from atop the Summit Ridge! Since God has taken such extreme care in His array of these things, how much more care has He put into each of us individually, as human beings, His highest order of creation on the planet earth? How utterly fortunate we are to stand on this Summit Ridge where we can physically see and spiritually contemplate each of these things and all of these things.

How honorable it is to be able, if we are indeed able, to touch a great rock or even a small one! How satisfying to scoop up a handful of fine pebbles and grains of sand from your foot trail and sift them through your fingers! How comforting to feel the wind atop this high place! How artistically harmonious are the wind-shaped Bristle Cone Pine, the Lodge Pole, Jeffrey, Sugar, White Fir and the towering Ponderosa!

There are also within view here a variety of green and flaming yellow fern, which smother the banks of a melodious creek that winds among a great mixture of boulders and exquisite thickets of manzanita! There is the distinctly sharp scent of sage and incense cedar! At this elevation the sky overhead is a fierce blue, the air pure and clean—who cannot know that the hand of the Lord has done all this? (Job 12:9)

The wise man or woman who has studied God's Word, who has increased in faith and believed in His promises, who has ascended to the Summit Ridge in their faith, having seen the unseen attributes of God through the things He has made—he or she indeed stands near the very pinnacle of faith! He or she understands, in great depth, the value of God's creation and can take any part of it anywhere with them in their heart or picture it within their mind. He or she can use it to fight temptation, to sustain themselves through hard times, to be thankful in good times and to truly praise and honor God at all times. He or she can find great satisfaction and incomparable joy in teaching, helping and encouraging others.

If you have come this far in your faith, if you have reached the Summit Ridge, then you have indeed conquered many things. You have spiritually discovered the variety of talents which God has endowed you with for this very purpose. The peace of God, which surpasses all understanding, can become available to you (Philippians 4:7). This mature faith and trust can lead you confidently across the ridge and to the actual summit of the Mountain of Believing.

The summit of true believing is *putting your belief into action*. That *is* the pinnacle of faith. True belief will allow you to put yourself in your own place and to put God in first place, which is on the front line, first and foremost in your life—in your thoughts, in your words and in your deeds. True belief will allow you to walk with God as His friend. True belief will allow you to understand the more important inner needs of others and to freely give your life to and for them, as Jesus did.

It will allow you to give generously of the things God has so freely given to you: Compassion, Mercy, Forgiveness, Patience, Kindness, Gentleness, Meekness and Self-control. This is the fruit of the Spirit of God within you. This is love—the mind of Christ within you—the greatest attribute and the very greatest commandment of God. Indeed, welcome to the Mountain of Believing! Your many failures are no longer a problem because you have put your trust in God—your life, hopes and dreams into His hands.

You have accepted who you are. You can now experience for the first time *true freedom*. You are therefore no longer a scumbag, wallowing in the mire. Though you will continue to fail in one way or another, you have finally discovered what it is to be a child of the Most High God. And when the Lord returns, you will be made *perfect*—there will be no more failures.

*

Have you learned to respect the Lord of creation? Where are you on the spiritual Mountain of Believing? Are you at Base Camp? Have you started the Early Ascent? Are you somewhere on the North Face (rock of promises)? Have you climbed to the Summit Ridge? Have you crossed that narrow spine toward the Summit itself? Wherever you are, be sure that you take into view all that is around you. Share your discoveries in truth with others along the way. Live free, help the world to truly see God, and trust in your Creator.

Be patient in this endeavor. God in His own time will lift you up and you will know and can rest in the fact that He can indeed do all that He has promised! When you are out there hiking, respect everything that moves—even the tiniest of creatures. Respect everything you touch—especially those little pebbles underfoot, or that blade of grass you might pick up and hold in your hand. Be consistent out there as well—occupy your time honoring God through appreciating His creation. Become one with Him.

Thanks for hiking with me on the Mountain of Believing. It is hoped that your journey has been one of illumination. May God enrich your spirit as you continue *Hiking the Trail of Truth*. I most sincerely hope to hear from you regarding your discoveries. I am not one of those authors that you cannot get hold of. You can reach me through e-mail at, hikemark@hotmail.com, or contact me via my trail phone, currently, 909-549-0068. I will respond to you immediately upon receiving your communication.

I hope I was able through this writing to shed some light on your path. I hope that you can find your spiritual home—your connection with God. I hope that you have truly learned to respect the Lord. I hope also that you can begin to see the supernatural through the natural. You have a map and compass now, and I hope that you will choose to share these things with others. May God bless you.

Sincerely, *Mark S Taylor*

Epilogue

He raised me up, so I could stand on mountains...

Today, I was sitting on top of a large granite boulder, overlooking a spacious valley. It's a desolate area, not far from home. I was reflecting on life, something I have done quite often during these last months while weaving this writing together. I was having a difficult time keeping my pipe lit in the wind.

It reminded me that somewhere along the road of life I found that I was dead, and struggled many years thereafter to come back to life again. I recalled at that moment one time when my son, Mitch, was very young. We made a batch of cookies, placed them in a cookie tin, and walked together down a long, steep hill in the Ohio country to deliver them to a poor and needy family, whom we didn't even know.

When we knocked on the door a man poked his head outside. I told him that we had brought his family some cookies. He soon opened the door and allowed us to enter. The family was quite delighted with our gift, and we stayed and visited with them for some time. I'll not forget the feelings I had then, nor the warm emotions expressed by that family. I have come to realize that those feelings and emotions are life at its fullest. As I sat atop that boulder I began to wonder why my mind would suddenly bring to remembrance something like that. Now I know why:

My most crucial advice to you in your search for or walk with God, in spite of the stains of your sins, is that you learn to understand that you have great significance to Him. Whether you have great earthly accomplishments or seemingly no accomplishments, whether you are President of the United States or homeless on some lonely street in the filthiest part of town— you are important to God. He has given you many things of which you are the steward. How you handle any and all of these things is all summed up in stewardship.

All things belong to God. He has only allowed you their use. You need to allow this truth to become your guide to daily living. The Bible is full of heroes, both great and small, some so small that only one sentence in the entire one thousand one hundred eighty-nine chapters of the Bible is devoted to them, and many of them are unnamed. They are listed as "a certain man" or "a certain woman," or described in another way without name.

Yet, their contribution to God is significant enough to be mentioned by the Holy Spirit of God, who inspired the writers of the Bible to include their faith in the narrative. Some are mentioned only as "others" who did this or that, and are listed in faith's grand hall of fame (Hebrews, chapter 11). You can be a part of that list as well.

You may have come a long way in life, not knowing if you have ever done anything worth the Lord's attention. You may have accomplished something for Him, but amidst the struggles of life it seemed so insignificant to you that you have seemingly no memory or awareness of it. On the other hand, you may be a young person, just starting out in life, on fire for the Lord and expecting to accomplish great things. Whichever of these you are, God will use you only as He chooses. He may use you for great things or for just one, solitary small thing in your entire lifetime.

Bottom line—your life is not your own. God will form you as He wishes and will use you for His purpose, in His time, and what you do or have done with what you've been given will serve to glorify Him. That is His purpose for you. God can deal with your sins and He alone has the power to deal with them. Your personal efforts at anything or your failure in anything will neither enrich nor thwart his ultimate plan for you.

Trust then in Him alone. Don't depend on the world you live in and never trust in yourself. Let God lead. He will let you know that He is there, and will help you to serve others, conforming you into the image of His Son. You will find your fullest joy in Him, and in the end, eternal life. Would you like some better advice on top of the good advice? Acquaint yourself with the Psalms. One of my favorites is Psalm 25:

To You, O Lord, I lift up my soul. O my God I trust in You; Let me not be ashamed; Let not my enemies triumph over me. Indeed, let no one who waits on You be ashamed; Let those be ashamed who deal treacherously without cause.

Show me Your ways, O Lord; Teach me Your paths. Lead me in Your truth and teach me, for You are the God of my salvation; On You I wait all the day.

Remember, O Lord, Your tender mercies and Your loving kindness, for they are from of old. Do not remember the sins of my youth, nor my transgressions; According to Your mercy remember me, for Your goodness sake, O Lord.

Good and upright is the Lord; Therefore He teaches sinners in the way. The humble He guides in justice, and the humble He teaches His way. All the paths of the Lord are mercy and truth, to such as keep His covenant and His testimonies. For Your namesake, O Lord, pardon my iniquity, for it is great.

Who is the man that fears the Lord? Him shall He teach in the way He chooses. He himself shall dwell in prosperity, and his descendants shall inherit the earth. The secret of the Lord is with those who fear Him, and He will show them His covenant. My eyes are ever toward the Lord, for He shall pluck my feet out of the net.

Turn Yourself to me and have mercy on me, for I am desolate and afflicted. The troubles of my heart have enlarged; Bring me out of my distresses! Look on my affliction and my pain, and forgive all my sins. Consider my enemies, for they are many; And they hate me with cruel hatred. Keep my soul and deliver me; Let me not be ashamed, for I put my trust in You. Let integrity and uprightness preserve me, for I wait on You.

(Verses 1-21, NKJV)

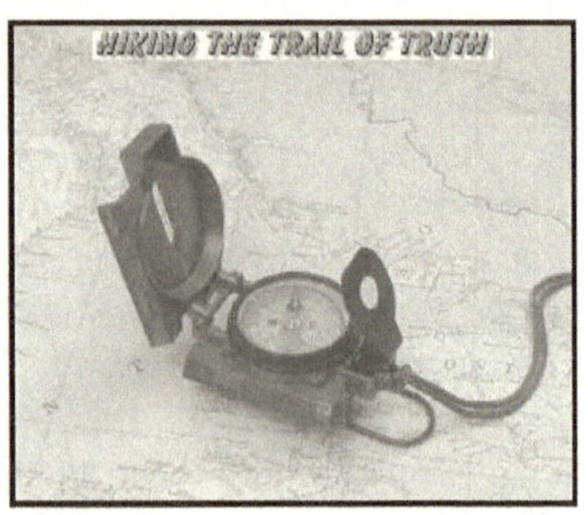

References and Notes:

Chapter 1

1. All information on Noah's Ark was made available through the author's personal contact with Ron Wyatt himself, and, Wyatt Archaeological Research, Cornersville, Tennessee, some of which is available on the Internet at wyattmuseum.com. Information was thoroughly investigated by the author in 1991, and is contained in the author's notes and on video.

2. Information based on author's personal research and notes.

3. Information based on author's personal exploration, research and notes.

4. Information based on author's personal research and notes.

5. *The Mountain of God*, the discovery of the real Mt. Sinai, Robert Cornuke and David Halbrook, copyright by Bob Cornuke, 2000, Broadman & Holman Publishers, Nashville, Tennessee, p1, 75,85,125.

6. Information based on author's personal observation, research and notes.

7. All information on The Ark of the Covenant was made available to the author through Ron Wyatt himself, and, Wyatt Archaeological Research, Cornersville, Tennessee, some of which is available on the Internet at wyattmuseum.com. Information was thoroughly investigated by the author between 1991-99, before Ron Wyatt passed away, and is contained in the author's notes and on video.

8. Some years after Ron Wyatt passed away, part of his recorded work regarding the Ark of the Covenant was removed from public circulation. Since he passed away before he could return to the site, critics complained that he was unable to offer proof of his discoveries in the lower chamber, which held the Ark. I submit that his critics should have read between the lines— Wyatt's story is proof enough. After all, his discovery confirms that Christ's atonement for sin was a reality and done according to God's Law. It also proves that God's wisdom is greater than man's, and that He accomplishes things in a way not foreseen by men. To the believer, Wyatt's discovery makes absolutely perfect sense. Come, let us reason together; the discovery related in the story itself is absolute proof of the story itself—no if's, and's or but's about it.

Chapter 2

1. *In The Beginning*, Compelling Evidence for Creation and the Flood, Walt Brown, PhD., Seventh Edition, copyright by Walt Brown, 2001, Center for Scientific Creation, Phoenix, Arizona; used for teaching by permission, p31.
2. Author's notes, Ohio Valley Christian Lectureships, 1976-78
3. Several generations after the flood, multiple languages began at Babel (Genesis 11:1-9). The name Babel gives us our word "to babble," meaning, "to utter meaningless sounds." Most scholars place Babel's location somewhere between today's Tigris and Euphrates Rivers, near the sight of ancient Babylon and the mountains of Ararat, where Noah's Ark landed (Genesis 8:4).
4. Author's notes, A Special Study on the Great Flood, Sunset Extension School, Lubbock, Texas, 1991
5. Author's notes, Ohio Valley Christian Lectureships, 1976-78**6.** Author's notes, The Flood and Science Documentary featuring Dr. Walt Brown, Church of Christ, Temple City, California, 1991. This information is also available from reference #**1**, part 2, beginning p85.
7. The Flood record, Genesis 7:17 thru 8:14
8. Genesis, chapter 1, verses 2, 6, 7, 9, 10, 20, 21 and 22. Water is used in performing miracles throughout the entire Bible.

Chapter 3

1. Genesis 9:12 thru 17. As long as it remains, the earth will never again be completely destroyed by water. The present heavens and earth are instead reserved for destruction by fire on the final Day of Judgment, after which new heavens and a new earth will be formed, according to God's promise, 2nd peter 3:5 thru 13.

2. 1st Corinthians 3:18-21. Men are foolish in their theories regarding the geophysical earth and the solar system. God first created all things full grown; therefore determining age is impossible, save carbon dating, which was made possible by the Great Flood and accounts for history after the flood, a mere 5000 years ago. No accurate dating beyond that time period is possible and scientifically confirmed as impossible. Paleontologists and geologists are among the worst offenders of this truth. See also in reference to dating: *In The Beginning*, Compelling Evidence for Creation and the Flood, Walt Brown, PhD., Seventh Edition, copyright by Walt Brown, 2001, Center for Scientific Creation, Phoenix, Arizona; used for teaching by permission, p244-246.

3. Public information made available from Death Valley NationalPark, Death Valley, California 92328.

Chapter 4

1. *In The Beginning*, Compelling Evidence for Creation and the Flood, Walt Brown, PhD., Seventh Edition, copyright by Walt Brown, 2001, Center for Scientific Creation, Phoenix, Arizona; used for teaching by permission, p5.

2. Information on the animals, birds and insects discussed in this chapter is the product of the author's research, studies in Job (Chapters 38 thru 42), and personal experience over several years.

Chapter 5

1. John 14:6 & 6:44,45, 1st Corinthians 12:3, Romans 8:14
2. Ephesians 6:12, Ephesians 2:2, Matthew 4:8,9, Revelation 12:10, Matthew 7:14, 2nd Timothy 4:7,8
3. Isaiah 1:8, Hebrews 8:12 & Romans 11:33 thru 36
4. 1st John 1:8 thru 10, Romans 8:26,27,34, Hebrews 7:25

shows us that these things are necessary elements in our comprehending the universe. Most importantly through all of this he educates us on how to attain true peace and contentment and then hold onto it throughout the storms of life—a most informative read!

(150 pages paperback & *available on Kindle*)

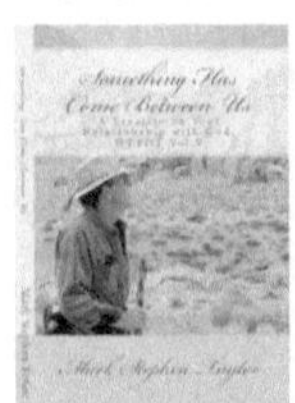

Something Has Come Between Us; (Hiking the Trail of Truth, Volume V) *A Treatise on Your Relationship with God.* It's time to hike another Spiritual Journey in the company of award-winning Christian author, Mark Stephen Taylor. *Something Has Come Between Us* is an in-depth look at our personal relationship with God. It is an eye-opening account of what has actually come between God and mankind. Within this volume the author helps us to better comprehend the seemingly endless plight of the human race, and gives us a deeper understanding of the forces of darkness that work against us.

Mr. Taylor says that the words 'something has come between us' should become a part of one's everyday thinking in our relationship with God. Why? Because, first and foremost, it will teach us humility —something very precious in the sight of our Creator. Humility is an *eternal principle*—something that each of us need to find and embrace.

The author indeed helps us to better understand the difficulties of this earthly life through this particular journey, and leads us along a most profound trail of discovery, illumination and hope. Hiking is a good thing—much can be gleaned along the trail. Don't be shy...come on along...let's do it!

(134 pages paperback & *available on Kindle*)

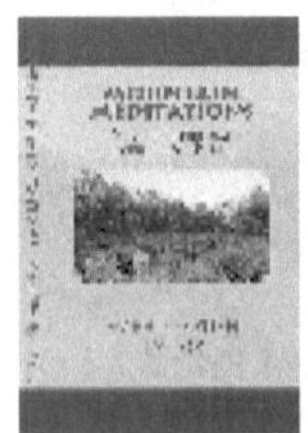

Mountain Meditations; (Hiking the Trail of Truth, Volume VI) *A Daily Spiritual Journey for Hikers.* In dealing with the busy world around us; with the serious business of living, of loving, with the sheer joy of discovery, of learning to give joyfully to others, or with deep despair, whether it be our own or that of a friend who needs a reason for living, Mountain Meditations gives you God's perspective. Every word is God Himself speaking about life and the role that He wants you to play in it. Special, eye-opening thoughts are presented for each day of the year, using words and verses from the Bible. Follow its directives and you will discover a lifestyle that is indeed rewarding.

(222 pages paperback *& available on Kindle*)

The Last Trumpet*;* (Hiking the Trail of Truth, Volume VII) *The Truth Concerning World End Events.* Warnings have many forms—lights, signs, sights, sounds, smells, feelings, and written words, as in the above text. With varied focus, their purpose is the same—to advise alertness and caution because of imminent danger. Responses to these warnings will also vary, from disregard and neglect to evasive or corrective action. How a person reacts to a warning is usually determined by the situation and the source. An impending storm is treated differently of course than an onrushing automobile, and the counsel of a trusted friend is heeded much more than the flippant remark by a stranger or the fearful guess of a child.

There are numerous warnings throughout the Scriptures. Second Peter is a letter of warning—from an authority none other than the courageous, experienced, and faithful apostle. And it is the last communication from this great warrior of Christ. Soon thereafter he would die, martyred for the faith.

This book, *The Last Trumpet*, is your warning, dear reader. A warning about the future—your future, my future, and the future of the world's entire population. Yet, this most dire warning is followed by a precious promise—an extremely hopeful one indeed. Read well and learn...

(68 pages paperback *& available on Kindle*)

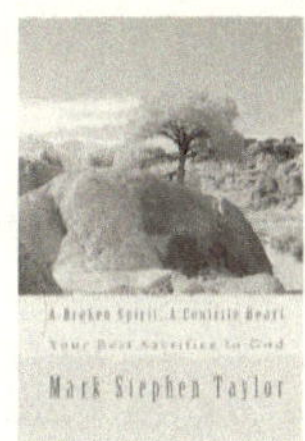

A Broken Spirit, A Contrite Heart (Hiking the Trail of Truth, Volume VII) These are indeed spiritual sacrifices, not physical ones as were required under the old law. Jesus of course made the ultimate sacrifice, yet we as individuals are required to make important sacrifices as well, which is why this book was written. Our most essential sacrifice? The psalmist makes it clear: "O, Lord open my lips, and my mouth shall show forth Your praise. For you do not desire sacrifice (physical) or I would give it. You do not delight in burnt offering. The sacrifices of God are a broken spirit, a broken and a contrite heart—These, O God, You will not despise (Psalm 51:15-17).

Let us hike this section of the trail of truth together, dear reader, and let us endeavor to understand the depth and importance of this particular sacrifice required of us...a broken spirit, a contrite heart...
(56 pages paperback & *available on Kindle*)

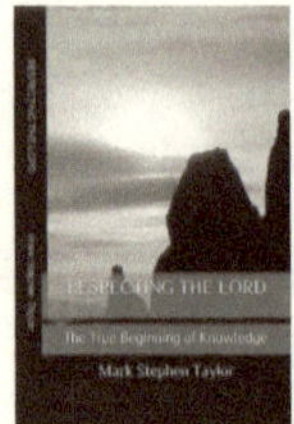

RESPECTING THE LORD (Hiking the Trail of Truth, Volume VIII) The True Beginning of Knowledge. There does not seem to be a predominant amount of respect for the Lord in these current times in which we live. Let's face it—it's a chaotic world out there, is it not? I would blame most of that on a lack of both teaching and understanding regarding the Creator of the world. However, the existence of God can be clearly seen through the things He has made, which things are quite obvious all around us Yet, it appears that many are not really looking. Why is that, I wonder?

It is written that a fear (respect) of the Lord is truly the beginning of knowledge (Proverbs 1:7). Here, Solomon is clearly teaching that belief in God is the necessary prelude to the understanding of solid truth and the acquisition of any knowledge. *Beginning* is literally first in order of importance; the first principle. In many Biblical passages the fear (respect) of the Lord is to be taught and learned. The beginning (foundation) of all true knowledge is grounded in this respect.

The purpose of this particular writing is to teach one how and why to respect the Lord. It is an eye-opening hike along the trail of truth which can give understanding to the simple—to those of contrite heart. To anyone who has the ability to reason this journey will be quite profoundly informative. This journey requires courage—the personal will to reach the summit of the mountain of believing. We are hoping, dear reader, that you are one of those rare persons...
(146 Pages paperback & *available on Kindle*)

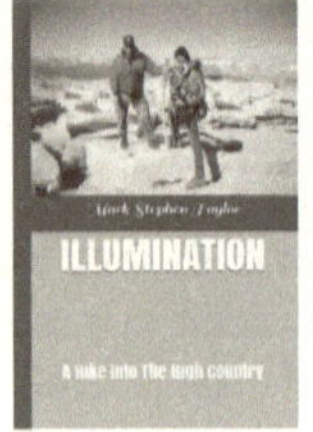

ILLUMINATION (Hiking the Trail of Truth, Volume IX) A Hike into the High Country; ILLUMINATION, a Hike into the High Country, is the exhilarating story of searching for, discovering, and attempting to fulfill a purpose in life—your individual purpose. It can indeed be a most illuminating trek—if you're willing.

Have you ever hiked the high places of the earth? Have you trekked through the deserts of the American southwest, or hiked among the formations in our many National

Parks? Hiking can be quite inspirational and is good for you physically as well. Consider if you will that the human brain is more complex than any man-made computer will ever be. It can allow you some profound discoveries that have not yet surfaced—but in time could... Your trek through this particular writing may indeed be the most illuminating adventure of your lifetime...

Are you ready? Hang on tight! The greatest thing about this most descriptive author is that as you turn the pages, you will find yourself right there in the middle of it all—living and breathing the story, and perhaps find yourself gleaning essential and purposeful understanding...

(86 Pages paperback & *available on Kindle*)

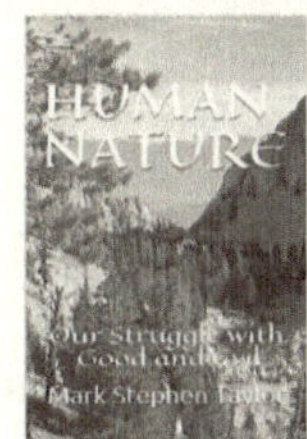

HUMAN NATURE; Our Struggle with Good and Evil; (Hiking the Trail of Truth, Volume VIII). The purpose of this book is to help you, dear reader, to understand human nature and our ongoing, individual struggle with good and evil—help you to know just who you are and what you will need to learn in order to deal with yourself as a human being. It will be a difficult journey—yet it is indeed an insightful and most needful trek. However, there are many who care very little about this journey— many who fail to acknowledge the deceitfulness of human nature— especially their own. It requires an unwavering pursuit of honesty in order to take an in-depth look at one's self—a rare endeavor in this present world. Do you, dear reader, have the quality that it takes to make that endeavor? If at this time you do not, it can be developed, if you are willing.

(82 Pages paperback & *available on Kindle*)

Author's Favorite:

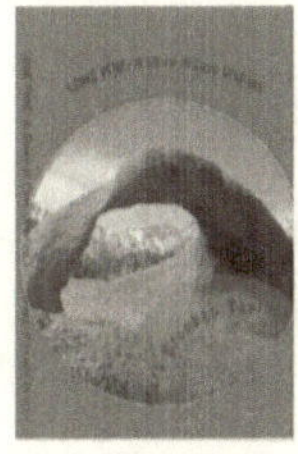

LONE PINE (Present Day Fiction); *A Story of Love Undying*; There are those who truly know what love is all about, and there are those who do not. This is a tragic yet incredibly heartwarming story about those who do. Narrated by Stands With The Bear of the Shoshone Nation, you are about to embark on a journey into the lives of four very intimate friends, who make their abode in Lone Pine, California; home of Mt. Whitney, highest mountain in the contiguous United States, located in the bold, majestic range of the High and mighty Sierra-Nevada.

This story takes you from the very beginning of their rewarding journey together, to probing into the incredible depth of their individual lives, and highlighting their most profound adventures into reality as a group. It is a story of how they eventually become one in spirit, and soar as individuals into a unique realm of understanding and bond of love that few humans ever experience, yet would surely grab onto the opportunity to do so. Accordingly, this knowledgeable perception of love is truly obtainable.

From award-winning author and explorer, Mark Stephen Taylor, this story of ordinary, careworn human beings, graciously transformed by the wonders of their environment, explores the diverse tragedies and rewards that come with self-discovery in the world in which we are all a part of. Taylor's writing style and insight are once again evident in this astonishingly down to earth tale of faith, hope and love undying. Come and hike along with his undisguised characters and see for yourself...

(244 Pages paperback & *available on Kindle*)

 **From the Lone Pine Western Series:**

A HIGH SIERRA CHRISTMAS (Old West Fiction); *An Untold Tale of Jeremiah Johnson*, Latest Holiday Edition. Are you looking for a unique gift item for friends or family this year? I am hoping that you will consider, *A High Sierra Christmas*; 'an untold tale of Jeremiah Johnson.' Most everyone wants to know what happened to Jeremiah up there in the Rockies. Is he up there still? No, he ain't—in fact, he later went into the High Sierras, and you can discover his illuminating fate in the pages of this new and non-traditional fiction tale of the American West. On Christmas Eve, you and yours can saddle up, ride into the majestic High Sierra scenery (full page photo at each chapter), and actually become a part of the story!

(182 pages paperback & *available on Kindle &* **audio** *version*)

Three Days In LONE PINE (Historical Old West Fiction); *An Untold Tale of The High Sierra, 1873.* Do you believe in angels? In 1873 the town of Lone Pine, California came to believe in them. Lone Pine is the home of Mt. Whitney, highest mountain in the contiguous United States, towering some 14, 497 feet. The white granite range of the High Sierra has been around for several thousand years, its towering spires unique in North America. However, the first recorded climb to this peak was not until August 18th, 1873, when three local fishermen braved the lofty crags and reached its elusive summit.

Prior to that, there had been many attempts, but recorded history tells us those climbers who made the attempts never ended up on the right peak! Some of them did not return, and were never heard from again. Hundreds of peaks point skyward in this range of mountains, and though Mt. Whitney is the highest, it remained the most elusive for decades. But Indian legends tell of evil spirits that once made their abode atop this very mountain. From this great height it was believed that these dark forces planned their wicked strategies against our entire country. It was their mountain!

The Indian legends also foretold of a time when the evil would be no more; a time when men and women would freely hike the mountain and experience the wonder and exhilaration it could produce within one's spirit. According to those legends, and according to an old diary found in the hills just west of Lone Pine, that time did arrive. It was in August of 1873, when the most powerful leader of the angelic host paid an unannounced visit to the town. After his Three Days in Lone Pine, the mountain, the birds and the animals…even the people, would never be the same…

(212 pages paperback & *available on Kindle*)

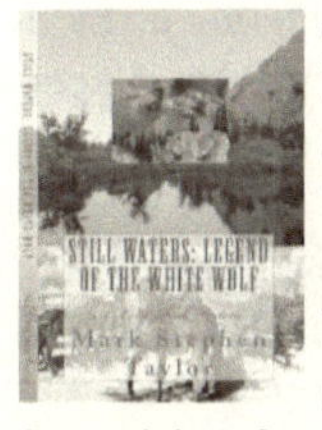

STILL WATERS: Legend of the White Wolf (Old West Fiction); Welcome to another Lone Pine Western by award-winning author, Mark Stephen Taylor. STILL WATERS is a journey amidst the heartbeat of the High Sierra; Lone Pine California and Mount Whitney—the highest mountain in the contiguous U.S.A. This is a story of the great, white wolf, who in legend takes on the spirit of a Native American man and seeks to protect both the animals and the people of 1874 Lone Pine.

Within this writing a memorable cast of characters come to life, whose individual lives are changed for the better through their confrontation and association with the legendary white wolf. Journey with them now to the Still Waters of Serrano Ridge—your own life may turn out to be much richer for it.

(156 pages paperback & *available on Kindle, &* **audio** *version*)

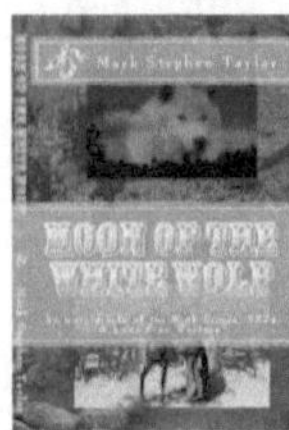

Moon of the White Wolf (Old West Fiction); *An Untold Tale of The High Sierra, 1874.* Welcome to another Lone Pine Western by award-winning author, Mark Stephen Taylor. Moon of the White Wolf, an untold tale of the High Sierra, 1874, is a journey amidst the heartbeat of the High Sierra; Lone Pine California and Mount Whitney—the highest mountain in the contiguous U.S.A. This is a continuation of the legend of the great, white wolf, first introduced in the author's work, Still Waters: Legend of the White Wolf.

In this enduring sequel, the town of Lone Pine and surrounding ranches, as well as the village of the Shoshone, are threatened by an attack from the Paiute tribe to the south. This of course disrupts the ordinary lives of the story's characters, but when the great white wolf returns to the area under a harvest moon, there is indeed great hope. However, not all believe in the legendary white wolf. Yet, during the human struggle for understanding, a memorable cast of characters lives are brought together in an unforgettable way in this great story of the early west. The outcome is most profound. Enjoy!

(162 pages paperback & *available on Kindle &* **audio** *version*)

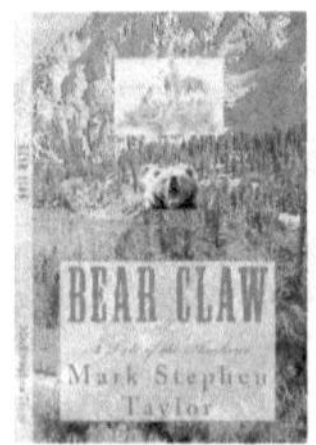

Bear Claw is the renown Chief of 1870's Lone Pine California Shoshone in the author's 'Lone Pine Western Series', which stirring arrangement includes; "Three Days in Lone Pine", "Still Waters, Legend of the White Wolf", and, "Moon of the White Wolf". Readers of this most enlightening series of the Old West have expressed a desire to know more about Bear Claw—his roots, his upbringing, and details of the man's life prior to his first appearance as the aged and all-wise

Shoshone Chief in, "Three Days in Lone Pine", first published in 2010.

This particular edition of the series will attempt to satisfy that compelling desire, while at the same time bring to life an informative tale of Lone Pine's early days and the alluring characters that were a part of it. Lone Pine, just below the great Mt. Whitney, is indeed a unique place—even to this day. This historic California town of the old west is nestled among vast and colorful standing rock formations, where numerous pinnacles reach toward the sky in an awesome display.

The author's well-written and notably descriptive tales do indeed come to life amidst the breathtaking landscape of the Mt. Whitney region. This most picturesque area has been used quite frequently as a scenic backdrop by the motion picture industry for over eight decades. And now, from this awe-inspiring backdrop, the author brings forth to his readers one of the most captivating tales in the Lone Pine Western Series...

(140 pages and available on Kindle)

From the *Lone Wolf Limited Mystery Series* comes these four great tales of mystery and adventure...

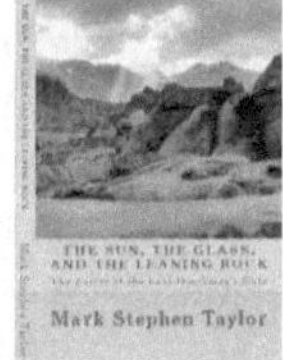

The Sun, The Glass, and The Leaning Rock (Fiction); *The Secret of the Lost Dutchman's Gold*, (#1 in the Mystery Series) is a daring tale of high adventure. The story opens in the year 1984, but centers on the 1924 discovery of the 'Lost Dutchman's mine' in Arizona, the inevitable misfortune of its discoverer, and the strange fate of the loot itself. A treasure map, an unusual necklace, and a simple nursery rhyme set the stage for double murder, betrayal, kidnapping, and unrelenting drama in this tale of the high desert!

(204 pages paperback & available on Kindle Available also in a 242 page paperback, large print edition, under its original 1984 title; 'A Second Chance'; a daring tale of high adventure.)

The Secret of Monument Valley (Historical Fiction); *The Trail of the Anasazi* (#2 in the Mystery Series), resolves the age-old mystery regarding the 1450 AD disappearance of the Anasazi people from their strongholds in the American southwest. Based on actual accounts from Native American residents of the Navajo Nation, award-winning author Mark Stephen Taylor thrusts his characters into the heart of this most interesting controversy. What they must endure is indeed most shocking. What they will find is most profoundly enlightening!

(176 pages paperback & *available on Kindle*)

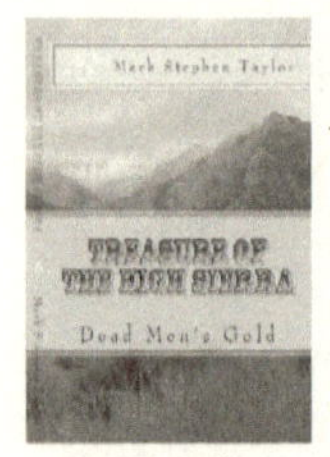

Treasure of the High Sierra (Historical Fiction); *Dead Men's Gold* (#3 in the Mystery Series):

Old Spanish gold—and pirate's treasure's...things like this usually arouse our interest—and for sure stir our imaginations. Mr. Taylor's 'Treasure of the High Sierra' is no disappointment in this regard...

In this 3rd mystery of the series, tracker & cartographer Mitch Holland and treasure hunter Rod Florea find themselves on Mt. Whitney (California), highest mountain in the contiguous USA. It is there that they come to the aid of two teenagers who are looking for hidden Spanish Gold. An old map purchased at a yard sale turns out to be quite authentic, and the 16th century pirate tale that gives the map that authenticity is indeed a bone-chilling account.

Kidnapping, murder, and a macabre pirate curse are only a few of the things that Holland and Florea must deal with as they take on this challenge atop the high mountain. Elite members of the Forest Service are also involved, along with the families of the two teenagers (Billy Brandt and Riley Taylor). Then there are the troubled spirits of pirates long dead...

(146 pages paperback & *available on Kindle*)

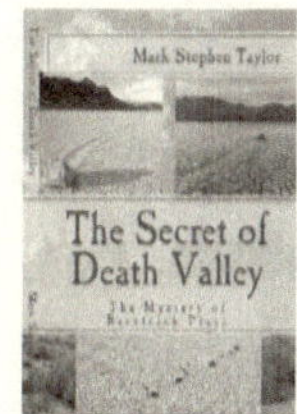

The Secret of Death Valley (Historical Fiction); The Mystery of Racetrack Playa (#4 and final in the series); Death Valley is a remote desert area located in eastern California. Situated within the Mojave Desert region, it features the lowest, driest, and hottest locations in all of North America. Badwater, a basin located within the Valley, is the specific point of the lowest elevation, at 282 feet below sea level. This area is only 84 miles east-south-east of Mt. Whitney, the highest point in the contiguous United States, with an elevation of 14,497 feet.

One of the most interesting and challenging mysteries of Death Valley is the sliding rocks at 'Racetrack Playa' (a playa is a dry lake bed). These rocks can be found on the floor of the playa with long and distinct trails behind them. Yes, that's right—and no one knows for sure how these rocks move, and no one has ever reported actually seeing them move—but they do move great distances, some of them weighing several hundred pounds!

Treasure hunter Rod Florea and tracker/cartographer Mitch Holland are about to confront this mystery—as they go in search of Spotted Elk, a Native American friend (The Secret of Monument Valley), who while on a personal quest has suddenly turned up missing in the far reaches of Death Valley—somewhere within the parched and desolate region known as Racetrack Playa...

Are you ready? Hang on tight! The greatest thing about this particular author is that as you turn the pages, you will find yourself right there in the middle of it all—living and breathing the story!

(142 pages paperback & *available on Kindle*)